ENDORSEMENTS

Suffice it to say that your pearls of wisdom had me laughing and crying as you drew me closer to the Lord. You have defined leadership, management, organizational development, and success in practical, biblical terms. And, it all comes from the heart of one who has achieved a lifetime of success in influencing others to move their lives and the organizations they impact to higher ground. I am so humbled to have you as a friend and partner in a ministry that is making a mark on our culture—a ministry that clearly has your fingerprints permanently embossed on the foundation! I long for some more of those great moments together!

—**Dr. Merrill Oster**
Founder and Chairman of the Board
Pinnacle Forum of America

Reading this book is like being at a fireside with a bigger-than-life hero who has just chosen you to be their personal friend. Ralph unpacks his life experiences in a direct and powerful demonstration of a most interesting life. After just a few pages, you will long to serve with greater humility, lead with passion, and love others like never before. I could not put it down!

—**Dr. Jon Sharpe**
President
C-3 Leaders

In our fifty-five years together, Ralph has influenced me, inspired me, and served as a role model of the kind of person "I would like to be when I grow up." And now, he has crafted a wonderful summation of much of what he has taught me. Ralph has presented, in this wonderful book, an incredible synopsis of much of his deep wisdom, character, and inspiration that has enriched so many of us that he has influenced through the years—a wonderful read as only he could present.

—**Ralph Bruksos**
Management Consultant

THOUGHTS FROM MY

★ Journey ★

THOUGHTS FROM MY
★ *Journey* ★

RALPH H. PALMEN

REDEMPTION
PRESS

Published by Redemption Press, PO Box 427, Enumclaw, WA 98022, Toll Free (844) 2REDEEM (273-3336)

Redemption Press is honored to present this title in partnership with the author. The views expressed or implied in this work are those of the author. Redemption Press provides our imprint seal representing design excellence, creative content, and high quality production.

Unless otherwise noted, all Scriptures are taken from the *Holy Bible, New International Version*®, NIV®. Copyright © 1973, 1978, 1984, 2011 by Biblica, Inc.™ Used by permission of Zondervan. All rights reserved worldwide. www.zondervan.com.

Scripture references marked NASB are taken from the *New American Standard Bible,* © 1960, 1963, 1968, 1971, 1972, 1973, 1975, 1977 by The Lockman Foundation. Used by permission.

Scripture references marked KJV are taken from the *Holy Bible, King James Version.*

ISBN 13:   978-1-68314-025-2 (Print)
                978-1-68314-026-9 (ePub)
                978-1-68314-027-6 (Mobi)
Library of Congress Catalog Card Number: 2016934875

DEDICATION

To Robert A. Funk, my co-worker, friend, business partner, and brother since 1965. Thanks for all the great times and laughs over the years! One of the great joys of my life has been helping grow Express Employment Professionals into the number one company in the United States in our field.

Acknowledgments

To my sister, Jerilyn Tyner, who has been an invaluable asset in getting this book ready to publish. I hope you will look up her books on the Internet and buy them. She is a great writer.

To my wife, Darlys, my children, Mark, Cheryl, and Todd, plus the greatest grandkids, Tayden and Olivia, for making my life such a joy!

And to all my friends who are too many to mention who have enriched my life and given me the gift of time and love.

CONTENTS

THE HIGHER ROCK

"Hear my cry, O God; attend to my prayer. From the end of the earth I will cry to you. When my heart is overwhelmed, lead me to the rock that is higher than I."

—Psalm 61:1–2

This has been a tough month. Lots of blood transfusions, pain, long nights, and a desire to give up—the feeling that I will be in heaven soon anyway, so let's get it done.

Then I went to the Rock. Last night I got more rest. Today I got up and read the Bible, wrote a devotional article, and then wrote out my goals for this coming year. I don't know what's coming my way in the days ahead, but I want to face it from the Rock that is higher than I.

There is a Rock that we can lean on, where we can find strength and power greater than ourselves. The Rock is there for all of us. We just need to reach out and touch the Rock.

Lord, today I pray for myself and all who are reading these words that You will lift me up to that Rock that is higher than I. May we see life not as we would see it, but as You do. May we operate with Your higher motives and goals. May we better understand Your plan and how You want us to live. Amen.

Are Your Seas Stormy?

"And a great windstorm arose, and the waves beat into the boat, so that it was already filling. But He was in the stern, asleep on a pillow. And they awoke Him and said to Him, 'Teacher, do you not care that we are perishing?' Then He arose and rebuked the wind, and said to the sea, 'Peace, be still.' And the wind ceased and there was a great calm."

—Mark 4:37–39

Have you ever been at sea in a storm? It's a good lesson in how limited our control is over the circumstances in our lives. When the wind blows and the waves get high, how do you respond?

I have been there. My initial response has been much like the disciples, and I have been afraid. However, I have found that I have someplace to go for peace. In the midst of storms, I have learned to turn to Jesus. Even though the circumstances did not change immediately, my attitude did; I found peace in the storm and let go of the grip fear had on my heart.

How are you today, my friend? Are you experiencing storms in your life? Are you struggling with fear about your current circumstances? Ask Jesus to give you peace in your heart. He will help you face your fears and get through whatever you are facing. The great lesson of storms is that we can face them with God's help.

GROWING STRONGER

"But those who wait on the LORD shall renew their strength; they shall mount up with wings like eagles. They shall run and not be weary; they shall walk and not faint."

—Isaiah 40:31

It is painful to look down and see your body wasting away.

When I was nineteen years old, I entered the Lewis Clark Valley weightlifting champion contest. The auditorium was filled with strong men from all over the area. The competition was based on how much weight you could lift in the curl, the bench-press, and the dead lift. Your total combined weight was then divided by how much you weighed.

I lifted a total of 625 pounds, and I weighed 129 pounds at that time. I won the title as The Strongest Man in the Lewis Clark Valley.

Today, due to the ravages of cancer, my body is no longer what it once was, but my spirit—the real me—is stronger than it's ever been. The truths in the Bible are not all about the physical world. It's the spiritual part of life that really matters.

Are you growing stronger each day in the spiritual things of life?

His Righteous Hand

"Fear not, for I am with you. Be not dismayed for I am your God. I will strengthen you, yes, I will help you. I will uphold you with My righteous right hand."

—Isaiah 41:10

What a great promise that the holy God who created the universe is concerned about us as individuals. He will strengthen us for the trials and challenges of our lives.

When I was a junior in high school, I signed up for a public speaking class. I gave two or three speeches, and each time, I thought I would die. My head got dizzy, and my stomach ached. I thought, "This is not for me," and I talked my way into switching to a shop class.

At this time, I have given 2,500 professional speeches. People might ask me, "What happened to your fear?" I still have it. But I have learned that God will strengthen me. He taught me that when I focus on myself and what people think of me, I have fear. When I think about the audience and pray God will use me to help them, the fear disappears.

What do you fear, my friend? With God, no river is uncrossable, no mountain too high. His Word assures us in Matthew 19:26 that with God, all things are possible. Let Him uphold you with His righteous hand and do some great things!

The Golden Rule

Do unto others as you would have them do unto you.

When we started Express Employment Professionals, one of our founding principles was that we would be a franchise-friendly franchisor. This basically meant to live by the Golden Rule in the way we treated the franchise owners.

As a result, our franchise agreement was fair and just. It protected the franchisee's rights as well as the franchisor. Our franchise agreement would be as simple as possible and provide protection for both parties. Our commission splits and territory assignments would allow for franchise owners to make a good living and build their business to whatever heights they were capable of. We would provide a plan and ongoing training to insure the success of the franchisee, as long as they did what we told them. We would settle any disputes with the franchisee in a fair and equitable manner.

The results have been a testimony to the value of building a business on Bible principles. We have had great relationships with our franchise owners, limited disputes, and prosperity for all. Express is now the largest company in the US in our field. Our company is like a big family, and God is blessing us.

Whatever your business is, are you following the Golden Rule in your dealings? When you treat your business associates and employees as you would like to be treated, you will find good results in your endeavors.

FINDING GOD'S DIRECTION

Lord, what shall I do, and where shall I go?

Sometimes the present is very foggy, and the future is unclear. We are uncertain what steps to take. What can we do to move forward? Do what is before you. If the barn needs painting, paint the barn. If the lawn needs mowing, mow the lawn. If there are calls that need making, make the calls.

Look for someone you can help. There is always someone who needs what you can give, even if it's just a smile, a prayer, or an encouraging word.

Pray for God's direction. Ask yourself if you are currently doing everything God has told you to do. A failure to obey His known will often blocks our understanding of His next step for us.

For example, praying for financial success without doing what we know we should do will not get us very far. If we pay our tithe and give as God directs us, we will give Him the opportunity to guide us in our finances.

God has a plan for your life that is more wonderful than you can imagine. Learn to live in obedience to God's will each day, and He will lead you to your future. After a lifetime, I am totally convinced that God has a wonderful plan for your life. He wants to guide and direct you; however, we need to demonstrate our willingness to obey.

DON'T PARK HERE

I once heard a sermon by an evangelist named William Fisher that has stayed with me my whole life. He said life is full of signs, one of which is "DON'T PARK HERE." Sadly, he said, too many people park where they shouldn't.

Some people park by their failures. They give up and quit trying. Don't park here.

Some people park by their success. They achieve something and park there. They stop growing and getting better. Don't park here.

Some people park by their sorrows. They let the bad things that happen to them stop them from growing. Don't park here.

Some people park at their handicaps. Don't let the unfortunate circumstances of life keep you from growing. Don't park here.

Some people park in the land of negativity. They see only what's wrong and never what is good. Don't park here.

If you are parking in any one of these spots today, don't park there. Start your engine and move to a more positive place, and then keep on going forward.

FOLLOWING JESUS

"Then a certain scribe came and said to Him, 'Teacher, I will follow
you wherever You go.'"

—Matthew 8:19

Where He leads me I will follow,
Where He leads me I will follow,
Where He leads me I will follow.
I'll go with Him, with Him
All the way!

These words from a great old hymn, *I Can Hear My Savior Calling,*
(1894) come flowing through me as I try to sleep. I want to be what
Jesus wants me to be. I want to go where He wants me to go. May
the testimony of my life be that I followed Jesus.

What about you, my friend? Who or what are you following? It
is easy to follow the crowd. It is easy to follow our selfish wants and
desires. It is easy to follow the influence of others. You have to purpose
and resolve to follow Jesus every day if you are going to become what
He wants you to be. Following Jesus is a good choice to make.

It Is Well

"Please run now to meet her, and say to her, 'Is it well with you? Is it well with your husband? Is it well with the child?' And she answered, 'It is well.'"

—2 Kings 4:26

Perhaps one of the great tests of our faith is to be able to say, "It is well," when it would appear that it really isn't.

In this story, the woman looked after the needs of the prophet Elisha. She set up a room for him in her house where he could stay when he was in her part of the country. She fed him and showed him great hospitality. The Bible says she was a notable woman.

In return for her kindness, God granted her a son. One day, after working in the fields with his father, her son came in with a bad head ache, and he died in his mother's arms. She laid him on his bed and went to find the prophet. When Elisha saw her coming, he sent his servant to meet her and ask how her son and husband were, and she replied, "It is well." When she reached the prophet, she fell at his feet and told him the problem. He returned with to her home and raised her son back to life.

When we face our darkest hours do we say with the Shunammite woman, "It is well?" Do we have enough faith in our heavenly Father that we know He will take care of us in a way that we can really trust Him?

The closer we build our relationship with God, the better we are able to trust Him in the darkest moments of our lives.

AM I TRULY THANKFUL?

"Giving thanks always for all things to God and the Father in the name of our LORD Jesus Christ."

—Ephesians 5:20

One of the significant differences between people is the way they respond to the circumstances of life. Some folks seem to be unhappy with everything. They are even suspicious of the good things that come into their lives. Others find joy and are thankful, as the Bible teaches, in all things.

Last night I had a wrong number phone call. The caller asked for Pat. I said I was sorry, there's no Pat here and that my name was Ralph Palmen. As it turned out, the caller was a man I had found a job for thirty years ago. We wound up having a wonderful chat. He told me he was now seventy-seven years old, and he was thankful for every day God had given him. What a wonderful gift it was to me to have had a wrong number call.

One time I was speaking at a church over a weekend, and one of the laymen let me stay at his house. We had dinner together, and I learned he that was in the real estate business. I asked how he chose real estate as a career. He replied, "It was because of the elephants; they got me fired." He went on to explain that he worked at a zoo as a young man. Once he forgot to lock the elephants' cage, and when they got out, he was fired. It turned out to be a blessing since he wound up taking a job selling real estate and became a very successful salesman and developer.

Are you thankful for *all* things? When you have a grateful and thankful heart in all things, your life is more pleasing to God.

I am thankful that you are reading this devotional.

WHO WILL YOU BECOME?

"Beloved, now we are the children of God; and it has not yet been revealed what we shall be, but we know that when He is revealed, we shall be like Him, for we shall see Him as he is."

—1 John 3:2

When I was a boy, a man moved from back East to the town I lived in. He had a great passion to go deer hunting. When the season opened, he had his license and a gun and headed for the woods. He was back before the day was over with some farmer's goat tied to his car. A reporter saw him, and the next day his picture showed up in the newspaper with a story about the "great deer hunter." I think he moved away shortly thereafter.

Sounds funny, but do you know what it means to be a Christian? Do you have a clear idea what God intends your life to be? Research has shown that only a small percentage of Christians have a biblically-based worldview. We may have the same problem as the hunter, setting out to be something that we have not clearly identified.

Do you study the values of Jesus so that you know Him as He is, and that as a child of God, you are to be like Him? What are the values you are living today? It's good to put these in writing.

THE WHOLE DUTY OF MAN

"Fear God and keep His commandments, for this is the duty of mankind. For God will bring every deed into judgment, including every hidden thing, whether it is good or evil."

—Ecclesiastes 12:13–14 NIV

There are many ways and many things we can give our life to. I have known people who have given themselves for a business, a church, a noble purpose, or a selfish one. There are many ways you can pour out your life.

I have also stood beside many people and seen their dreams turn to ashes. When you give your life to serve things that have an endpoint, you will inevitably come to the end. This does not always occur in a way that produces joy and fulfillment.

According to the wisest man who ever lived, King Solomon, the only thing that really matters is to fear God and keep His commandments. There is no endpoint there.

OUR GREAT COMFORTER

"Blessed be the God and Father of our LORD Jesus Christ, the Father of mercies and God of all comfort, who comforts us in all our tribulations that we may comfort those who are in trouble, with the comfort with which we ourselves are comforted by God."
—2 Corinthians 1:3–4

Last night as I lay in my hospital bed, I was lonesome and tired. My body ached, and I was fearful over what the night would bring. What do you do, and where do you turn when you find yourself in that situation?

I turned to God, raised my hands, and prayed out loud for His help and mercy. He came to me and brought peace to my heart and comfort to my soul. I slept and rested well last night, and this morning I am filled with hope and looking forward to what I can do for Jesus today. Perhaps I can help someone else in their journey. I will surely find someone I can help lift their burden today.

Life is mainly froth and bubble
But two things will stand as stone—
Kindness in another's troubles,
Courage in your own. –Adam Lindsay Gordon (1833–1878)

My friend, do you know and walk with the Great Comforter?

YOUR THOUGHT LIFE

"Finally, brethren, whatsoever things are true, whatever things are noble, whatever things are just, whatever things are pure, whatever things are lovely, whatever things are of good report, if there be any virtue and if there be anything praiseworthy, meditate on these things."

—Philippians 4:8

Someone wrote a book that said you become what you think about all day long. One of my friends said that could not be true, or he would have turned into a girl when he was sixteen.

What we think about is important. It does impact your behavior and destiny in life. One of the great blessings God gave us is the ability to control our thinking. When we feed our minds good thoughts, as Philippians 4:8 urges us, we get good results. When we put garbage in our minds, we get garbage out. Negative thoughts in equals negative results out.

Dwell on the good things in life, and you will get more positive results. Ask yourself, "How can I improve my thought life today?"

What Causes You to Weep?

"Jesus wept."

—John 11:35

The first time I remember weeping was when my father died. I was in high school. I remember standing by his graveside on a cold, blustery spring day. My grief overcame me, and I began to sob. The tears and anguish flowed out of me, and I could not stop. I don't know how long I wept, but it seemed like a long time before I could gain control over the pain that was flowing out of my body.

Crying is different. I tend to cry easily. I have watched "chick flicks" with my wife in the past couple of years, and I sometimes cry at them. I cry at many things, but weeping is different. It comes from a much deeper source.

Does the vision of the lost and dying cause you to weep?

Do you weep at injustice and the plight of your fellow man?

Do you weep for those caught in the clutches of sin and self-indulgent living?

Do you weep for our country and pray that God will raise up leaders who are courageous and will lead us to godly ways and principles?

Do you ever weep at all?

THE OFFERING

"As Jesus looked up, He saw the rich putting their gifts into the temple treasury. He also saw a poor widow put in two very small copper coins. 'I tell you the truth,' He said, 'this poor widow has put in more than all the others. All these people gave their gifts out of their wealth, but she gave all she had to live on.'"

—Luke 21:1–4

Several years ago, I was speaking in a church about giving. After the service a woman came to me and said, "I know what you are talking about. When I was young, my husband abandoned me. He left me with a small boy and no means of support. I was devastated. I went to church on Sunday, heartbroken and discouraged. When the offering plate was passed, I looked in my purse. All I had in the world was a ten-dollar bill. I took it out and placed it in the offering and said, 'God, I guess You will have to take care of us now.' That is exactly what He has done.

"Through the years, God always provided for us. I always had what I needed to raise my boy. Today he is a fine young man. He is a Christian serving God in his local church, and he has a nice family. God has taken good care of us."

The principle of giving to God and trusting Him for provision in our lives never goes out of style. May God give us the faith of these women that we would totally trust Him with our lives.

THE BEAUTY OF RESTORATION

"And the LORD restored Job's losses when he prayed for his friends.
Indeed, the LORD gave Job twice as much as he had before."
—Job 42:10

The story of Job is very interesting. He is a great man who loses all his wealth and possessions. He is the most miserable of all men. His friends try to help him understand what he must have done wrong to deserve such a tragedy. God seems to have deserted him. He is engulfed in all kinds of introspection and turmoil and even told to "curse God and die."

Through it all, he keeps his faith in God, and finally he prays for his friends. The Bible is silent on what he asks God to do, but I sort of think he must have lifted them up to God and asked God to help them. Most likely, he asked God to bless them.

It is interesting that God prospered Job after he prayed for his friends. It could be that through his struggles he had learned to focus on others rather than himself. I think this story clearly teaches that God will bless us when we focus on blessing those around us!

THOUGHTS ON MARRIAGE

"Let the husband render to the wife the affection due her, and likewise also the wife to her husband."

—1 Corinthians 7:3

When I was a young man, my mother-in-law paid us a visit. It was a busy time in our lives. We had two small children, and I was struggling to build a business.

My mother-in-law took me aside one day and told me I should be doing more to help my wife. I thought to myself, "Are you nuts? I married her so she could help me, not so I could help her."

I was too young and stupid at that time to realize we were created to serve each other. The reason God used marriage as an example of His relationship to the church is because good marriages are built on a principle of serving and loving.

Unfortunately, it has taken me too many years to understand and apply this idea to my life. I always had a desire to be a good husband, and good follower of Jesus, and a good employer. I'm still learning that I need to serve better. I've been a slow learner, but I am still learning.

How about you, my friend? Are you on a journey of learning to serve others? Jesus once said, "If anyone desires to be first, he shall be last of all and servant of all." (Mark 9:35). Who are you serving today?

GOOD FRUIT

"Therefore every tree which does not bear good fruit is cut down and thrown into the fire."

—Luke 3:9

Throughout the Bible we are admonished repeatedly to be fruitful. Each of us is created with a different and unique set of talents, and we are all designed to produce certain fruit according to our abilities. To produce good fruit, we need to discover our unique design and then learn how to use those abilities to serve and enrich the lives of others.

A person gifted with artistic ability should develop their skills in such a way to bring beauty into creation, to tell a story that lifts up the spirits and aspirations of others. That would be good fruit.

My friends at Pureflix produce movies that are inspiring and teach truths that improve other's lives. They bear good fruit. Others in the movie industry produce films that have a destructive impact. They bear bad fruit.

Spend some time thinking about the fruit you are producing in your life. Write down your thoughts and study the lives of people who have yielded good fruit. Make sure your fruit tree is getting lots of water and fertilizer!

ATTITUDE TUNE-UP

"Let as many bond servants as are under the yoke count their own master worth of all honor, so that the name of God and His doctrine be not blasphemed."

—1 Timothy 6:1

I once had a boss who saw things a lot differently than I did. His background was accounting, and mine was sales. When things needed to be done, our approaches were very different. I would try to overpower him and get my way. Our working relationship was not much fun.

One day I was at a church men's retreat, and the speaker talked about how important it is for Christians to respect and submit to the authority we are under in our work.

I was convicted that I was not working that way. I prayed and asked God to forgive me for my attitude. The next time I met with my boss, we had an issue to deal with that I knew we would disagree on. But when we met to discuss it, I said, "You're the boss. I'll do whatever you want me to do."

Our relationship changed, and that was about the time my career went into high gear. My new attitude made me more attractive to employers.

What attitude and actions do you take to the authorities in your life? Do you need a tune-up?

Prayer First of All

"Therefore I exhort you first of all that supplications, prayers, intercessions and giving of thanks be made for all men; for kings and all who are in authority that we may lead a quiet and peaceable life in all godliness and reverence, for this is good and acceptable in the sight of God our Savior."

—1 Timothy 2:1–3

"It bothers me to hear people speaking with such disrespect about our president, even if we don't agree with him," said a friend of mine recently. He caused me to pause and take inventory of my speech and conversations. I was convicted in my heart that I have most likely been guilty of what was troubling him.

When things are bothering me, I have learned it is a good idea to see what God has to say about it. The Bible says we are to be in prayer and give thanks for those in authority over us. Why do I find this so hard to do when I disagree so strongly with the policies and direction they are leading us? I am finding I can pray for leaders, their health, and ask God to give them wisdom.

The whole concept of loving and caring for people who are different, who think differently, and act differently is perhaps the truest test of our spiritual maturity.

My friend, how does this subject resonate with you? Perhaps it's a good subject to talk about with trusted friends.

FINISH YOUR RACE

"I have fought the good fight, I have finished the race, I have kept the faith."

—2 Timothy 4:7

My son-in-law just finished running the New York City Marathon. I am proud of him because he finished the race. It takes a lot of discipline and character to run twenty-six miles. I don't know how many people start the race but don't finish. We don't hear much about quitters; it's those who finish who get the glory.

Our character is often defined by the way we persevere in situations where we feel like quitting. It is easy to give up on our relationships, our jobs, and our challenges. It is easy to give up on your church, your spouse, and your committee assignment. Every day we have situations and people we would like to give up on. Sometimes we even feel like giving up on our kids. We drop classes that are too tough and bail out of situations when the going gets rough.

People of character don't do that. They hang in there. They don't quit. They find a way when there is no way. They finish the race.

Christians should be people of character who finish what they start out to do. When we finish our race on earth, we will inherit a reward of righteousness. I am not sure what that means, but I do know that the rewards of finishing the race are many, and we often see them in our circumstances in this life as well.

Don't give up. Don't be a quitter. Finish your race.

ARE YOU LISTENING?

"Then Paul stood up, and motioning with his hand said, 'Men of Israel, and you who fear God, listen!'"

—Acts 13:16

Recently, two airline pilots intending to land in Minneapolis flew over the airport and wound up flying into Wisconsin. They were not listening to the air controllers who were desperately trying to speak to them. Everyone was shocked that they could be so distracted.

I don't know about you, but I have missed my turnoff more than once because I was not paying attention.

The question I'm asking myself this morning is, "Am I tuned in to Jesus? Am I listening to His voice and letting Him guide me each day?" My honest response is, "Not enough." Sometimes I listen to other voices. Too often I just listen to myself.

I want to be God's man. I want to do God's will in my life. I have asked Him to live in and through me. Why then do I so often fail to listen to His voice? I think it has to do with focus. Like those pilots, I lose my focus. I need to be more focused on listening. I do know His voice. It just takes a moment to pray, "Speak to me, and I will listen and obey." It seems the more I obey, the clearer His voice becomes.

My dear friend, are you tuned in and focused on God's voice today?

A STRONG HEART

"Wait on the LORD. Be of good courage, and He shall strengthen your heart; wait, I say, on the LORD."

—Psalm 27:14

I saw a cartoon one day that had two buzzards sitting on a tree limb. One was saying to the other, "I'm tired of waiting. Let's go kill something." Not sure about you, but this is how I feel sometimes. I just want to jump in and make things happen (not the kill part). When I talk with someone about problems that need solving, I get so anxious to start doing something, I can hardly sit in my chair.

I understand courage and action. Courage comes more easily to me. However, waiting is sometimes beyond my capacity to understand. I want to help God do things. Perhaps it takes a different kind of courage to wait on God. Maybe He wants to develop our faith to trust Him when we can't see how He is working in the situation.

Dear God, would you help me to be a man who is willing to wait on You—to be the man with the courage to believe You are working when things seem to be going so far wrong and so different from what I had planned? Lord, would you teach me to wait and have my heart strengthened?

THE SHADOW OF HIS WINGS

"Keep me as the apple of Your eye; hide me under the shadow of Your wings."

—Psalm 17:8

It is early morning, and I am getting ready to go to the airport and catch a commuter airplane. Two flights today and two flights tomorrow. Not my favorite thing to do, especially when the weather is not very good. I'm not afraid of flying; it's crashing that worries me!

I have spent a good many hours bouncing around in airplanes and wishing for the flight to be over. At those times, I often pray and ask God to keep me under the shadow of His wings. What a wonderful metaphor!

I can see Jesus praying over Jerusalem, saying, "How often I have wanted to gather you under my wings." I am there. I am willing and eager to have Jesus gather me under those strong wings. That is where I want to live. I don't ever want to get out from under His wings. I want to be the apple of His eye, sheltered and protected by His love and grace. There is nothing I want more.

I have felt His protecting wings surround me as I have walked through my life's journey. I just want to stay there, to live there, to be close to Jesus. When I am afraid, when I am lonely, when I am discouraged, it is to His arms I go for peace and comfort.

How about you, friend? Are you living in the shadow of His wings?

FOLLOWING THE CROSS

"And he who does not take his cross and follow after Me is not worthy of Me. He who finds his life will lose it, and he who loses his life for My sake will find it."

—Matthew 10:38–39

I was speaking at a conference in New Orleans when I was a young man. Our hotel was not far from the famous Bourbon Street. One of my fellow speakers and I decided to take a walk and check it out.

It was an eye-opening experience. My most vivid memory of that night was seeing a man lying in the gutter. He was drunk and dirty—a total wreck of a man. As I looked at him, I thought he was once some mother's pride and joy. How did he wind up here? Looking back, I am sure he responded to a call from something that was promising him a good time. Satan always shows you the joy up front, and you find out about the pain later on.

Jesus recruits people by offering them a life of self-denial, discipline, and hardship. Only later do you find out about the peace, joy, and fulfillment that come from following Him. Choosing the harder way is the path that brings the greatest joy in the end.

It is so easy to want pleasure and instant gratification, but self-denial and waiting always produce a much better story in the end. Follow the cross, give yourself away, and you never have to worry about winding up in a gutter on Bourbon Street.

Are You a Shrewd Businessman?

"So the master commended the unjust steward because he had dealt shrewdly. For the sons of the world are more shrewd in their generation than the sons of light."

—Luke 16:8

One day I was listening to an interview with Gene Autry. The reporter said, "Mr. Autry, you have a reputation as a shrewd businessman." Autry quickly replied, "Oh, I don't consider myself a shrewd businessman. I think a shrewd businessman is someone who wrings the last cent of profit out of every deal. I never do that. When I make a deal with someone, I always try to make sure I leave some money in the deal for the other guy. I find when I look out for him, he is always more likely to want to do business with me again."

Living by the values of Jesus should help us become the kind of businessmen who look out for the other guy. Jesus tells us, "He who is faithful in what is least is faithful also in much" (Luke 16:10).

Being a Christian ought to make us different in the way we do business. To please God, we need to make sure all our business deals are done with integrity and the kind of ethics that reflect honor to the Master of our lives.

Dealing with Temptation

"As obedient children, not conforming yourselves to the former lusts, as in your ignorance; but as He who called you is holy, you also should be holy in all your conduct."

—1 Peter 1:14–15

When I was young, I had the impression that older people no longer had to deal with temptation. I must not be that old yet. However, I have learned a lot more about where my temptations come from and what to do with them.

One type of temptation I deal with is produced by getting too tired. I don't take good enough care of myself and wind up low on fuel. In these times, I get tempted to indulge in self-pity and blame others for my circumstances. I need rest and encouragement. I have learned to surround myself with people who have the gift of encouragement. Playing golf or just being with these folks is a tonic for me. Reading and rest do wonders, too.

The second type of temptation is of a deeper, spiritual nature. This temptation is from the devil. It attacks the deeper flaws in my character. When I experience this type of temptation, I'm beginning to realize that it is because I am nearing spiritual breakthroughs or achievements. Satan knows the best ways to defeat me. This is when I need to draw closer to God and reach out to the prayer warriors in my life. I feel their prayers lifting me when I can't seem to lift myself.

Do you have temptations in your life and a plan to deal with them? We all need others who help us become what we want to be.

No, No, He Won't Let Go

"For I am persuaded that neither death nor life, nor angels, nor principalities nor powers, nor things present nor things to come, nor height nor depth, nor any other created thing shall be able to separate us from the love of God which is in Christ Jesus our Lord."
—Romans 8:38–39

The relationships the world builds tend to be temporary, conditional, and open to change. They are situational and subject to frequent emotional upheaval, and they tend to produce insecurity and a search for the next best thing. Earthly relationships are poles apart from the love that comes from God.

Isn't it great to know that God loves us in a totally different way. God never lets go of us. When we fail Him, He still loves us. When we fail others, He still loves us. When we fail ourselves, He still loves us.

God reaches down and lifts us up in our darkest hour. He is always there, and nothing can separate us from the love of God.

WHO'S IN CHARGE HERE?

"Both riches and honor come from You, and You reign over all. In Your hand is power and might. In Your hand it is to make great and to give strength to all. Now therefore, our God, we thank You and praise Your glorious name."

—1 Chronicles 29:12–13

One of life's great questions is, "Who's in charge here?" I remember when my little daughter looked me right in the eye, stamped her little foot, and tried to stake out a position that she was in charge of our relationship. It became painful for both of us, because I felt quite strongly that I was supposed to be in charge.

Recently, I sat next to a lady and her son in a restaurant, and it was painfully obvious she had lost that battle long ago. It was not a pretty scene. She seemed like an intelligent, well-educated woman, but her attempts to reason with her little guy fell on deaf ears. Sometime in his life he will have some hard lessons before learning he is not in charge. Unfortunately, he will cause a lot of pain to those around him before he learns that lesson.

David said, "Yours is the kingdom, God. It is Your strength and Your power we rely upon. We praise You, oh God. You are in charge." Even though David was the king of Israel, he acknowledged he was not in charge. No wonder God loved David and lifted him up.

My dear friend, is God in charge of your life? Have you given Him all of your heart, your mind, your possessions? Do you know who is really in charge here?

JESUS STOOPED DOWN

"So when they continued asking Him, He raised Himself up and said to them, 'He who is without sin among you, let him throw a stone at her first.' And again He stooped down and wrote on the ground."
—John 8:7–8

This passage of Scripture is familiar to most Christians. A woman is caught in adultery, and according to the Jewish law, she is to be stoned. Wanting to make an issue of her sin, the religious leaders brought her to Jesus and said, "In the law, Moses commanded us to stone such women. Now, what do you say?"

Jesus did a curious thing. He stooped down and wrote in the dirt. Why did He do that? Could it be that He was getting down to her level? She was still standing, but most likely she felt like dirt. When I have confronted the sin and bad things I have done in my life, quite frankly, I have felt like dirt.

As they continued to speak to Him on the issue, He stood up, and said if they were free from sin, then go ahead and stone her. As the truth sunk in, one by one they walked away. Then, Jesus said to her, "Go, and sin no more."

Living by the values of Jesus means we stoop down to where people live. We understand and bring mercy and forgiveness, balanced by truth, and this without judgment.

ARE YOU IN THE ROCK?

Rock of ages, cleft for me,
Let me hide myself in thee.
Let the water and the blood
From thy wounded side which flowed,
Be of sin the double cure,
Save from wrath and make me pure!

Do you ever miss singing the old hymns? They seem to have a much deeper message than many of the modern songs we sing. I like *Rock of Ages* because that is where I go when life gets difficult. This marvelous hold hymn was penned by a young English preacher named August Toplady. One night he was travelling through a gorge when he was caught in a storm. He found shelter in a rock along the gorge, and there he penned the words to the now famous song that was first printed in 1775.

Jesus is the Rock. It is the blood that flowed from His side that washes our sins away. His blood makes pure all the impurities of our lives. It is that blood that brings holiness into an impure world.

Are you hiding in that Rock today?

WORKING TOGETHER FOR GOOD

"And we know that all things work together for good to those who love God, to those who are called according to His purpose."
—Romans 8:28

Some people misunderstand this Scripture, thinking everything that happens in your life is supposed to be good. That is just not true. Some things that happen are just plain rotten. Even a positive thinker has to admit that.

What the Scripture really says is that those rotten circumstances work with other circumstances to bring good out of bad stuff if we are committed to letting God mold and shape our life into something that has value and meaning.

For example, getting fired is a lousy experience. Yet I know many who have told me, "Getting fired is the best thing that ever happened to me. I would have never made the changes in my life that produced such positive results if I had stayed in that job."

Whatever the circumstances are in your life, even those that look really bad, God can help you build a beautiful story out of the ashes of your failed plans and dreams.

The key is to let the God who made you keep molding you.

GIVE THANKS TO THE LORD

"Oh, give thanks to the LORD! Call upon His name; Make known His deeds among the peoples!"

—1 Chronicles 16:8

Last night was my grandson's little league baseball game. He was the leadoff hitter and started the game with a solid hit into right field. He was safe on a fielder's choice his second at bat. He walked his next time up and hit a single in his final at bat. It was fun to watch him. But the best part took place after the game. He made a beeline for his grandpa. He gave me a big hug. I told him he did a great job, and he told me thanks for coming.

There is something that takes place in those moments that makes life worth living.

It is the same way with God. He is watching us play in the game of life. When we run to Him and say, "Thanks for being there. Thanks for all you do for me," it delights the heart of God.

The act of giving thanks to our heavenly Father is what bonds us to the heart of God. It is a good thing!

THE ZEAL OF THE LORD

"For out of Jerusalem will go a remnant, and those who escape from
Mount Zion. The zeal of the LORD of hosts will do this."
—2 Kings:19:31

The situation in Jerusalem looked bleak. King Sennacherib of Assyria
had the city surrounded. They had destroyed Samaria and obliter-
ated the nation of Israel ten years previously, and now they planned
to do the same to Judah. He had given them an offer: surrender and be
relocated or die!

This pagan king did not take into account the zeal of the Lord.
When God says there will be a remnant, He will see that it gets done.
That night, the angel of the Lord visited the camp of the Assyrians
and put 185,000 men to death. The rest got up the next morning,
found the men dead, and withdrew to Nineveh. God left a remnant in
Jerusalem as He had promised.

Interestingly, when the disciples in the New Testament went to
Assyria to preach the gospel, there was an outpouring of repentance
and acceptance of the gospel. In fact, the Assyrian church was one of
the major forces in the spread of Christianity throughout the East.

We should seek to know God's will and join forces with the zeal of
the Lord. He will bless our efforts and actions as we honor Him.

ARE YOU A TIMID CHRISTIAN?

"For God has not given us a spirit of fear; but of power and of love and of a sound mind."

—2 Timothy 1:7

I just lost a golf match because I was too timid. I had a six-foot, downhill putt that I needed to make to win a hole. I saw the line and tapped my ball just right, except I was too timid. The ball stopped just short of the hole, and I lost.

Many times we come up short because we lack power. The Bible tells us God will give us a spirit of power. Are you interested in having more power in what you do and say? Get plugged in to our power source, the spirit of God.

I fear we live in an age of timid Christians. Too many of us are silenced by the spirit of intimidation the world has promoted. Christians are ridiculed and put down by popular culture in a way that makes us often fear being "one of those." There is nothing new about that. Look at Peter and the other disciples. They were unable to stand for Christ because they had a spirit of fear. It was on the Day of Pentecost that they got plugged in to the power source that gave them boldness to go out and change the world.

Imagine what God wants to do with your life. Get rid of the spirit of timidity, plug in to the power source, and God will do big things with you.

VIEWS ON ALCOHOL

"It is not for kings to drink wine, nor for princes intoxicating drink, lest they drink and forget the law and pervert the justice of the afflicted."

—Proverbs 31:4–5

I decided when I was nineteen that I would not drink. I had a boss one time say, "Ralph, you are smart. You don't drink. Every stupid thing I have done in my life I have done while I have been drinking."

I know this is a contrary view. I know many godly people who drink. But I have seen the high cost many of my friends have paid for a drinking problem. It strikes down men and women without warning.

Bathsheba, Solomon's mother, was giving him advice on how to be a good king when she included these instructions. She gave him some other good advice that he ignored, and it cost him dearly. No record is found if he took her advice on drinking.

All I can say is I am happy with the choice I made. I know I'd be writing a different story if I had let myself indulge in strong spirits. My friend, we all make our own choices, and I hope yours are good ones.

The Nature of God

"Moreover I will make a covenant of peace with thee, and it shall be an everlasting covenant with them; I will establish them, and I will set My sanctuary in their midst forevermore. My tabernacle also shall be with them; indeed I will be their God, and they shall be my people."

—Ezekiel 37:26–27

One of the reasons we need to study our Bibles is to help us better understand the nature of God. In this passage, we see God desires to have peace with us, He wants an everlasting relationship with us, and He wants to create a place for us: to grow us and have fellowship with us.

Peace is wonderful. I like it when I am at peace with the world around me. Peace comes into our lives when we surrender to God's leading and learn to live in harmony with His teachings. When I violate His teachings, I feel a war developing in my heart.

I like things that endure. Long-term relationships, familiar environments, and things I can count on always appeal to me. The concept of an everlasting relationship with the Creator of the world I find highly gratifying.

Growth and increase are wonderful things. Whenever God talks about the good things He wants to do for us, growth always finds its way into the dialog.

God also desires to be present with us. Sometimes I question my value. It helps to realize the God who created the world values me enough to want to be my personal God and have a relationship with me.

Fight or Surrender

Surrender. Give up. Give in. Those words have not been much of a part of my life. I think I was born a fighter. When I started grade school in a new town, I attracted the school bullies who would torment and beat up on me after school. I soon learned I had to fight back. I got good at it, and they went in search of easier prey.

I had an uncle who taught me to box. I got good at it. Through my school years, I got in a lot of fights. I would never back down or quit. In college I boxed with a trainer and coach who told me I was good enough to be a pro. It was not one of my life's goals, but I enjoyed fighting. I switched from using my fists to using other skills to tackle life's challenges.

Surrender to Jesus came for me in a church service one night. The preacher had told us we needed to surrender our will to Jesus. I wanted to be my own captain, but someone was speaking to my heart, and I went to the altar and surrendered my will and life to Jesus. He has been in charge since then. I have found that surrender to God's will is a daily activity. It's a good one; it makes a winner out of a loser. Have you surrendered to Jesus, my friend?

WALK WITH HIM

"Did not our heart not burn within us while He talked with us on
the road, while He opened the Scripture to us?"

—Luke 24:32

Can you think of anything better than walking with Jesus? He will
make your way much brighter. He will make your way much lighter.
Let Him carry your heavy load. Jesus can be your friend, your guide,
and your companion.

Are you walking with Him today? He will teach you and help you
become a better you.

Strengthening the Hands of Others

"And whosoever remaineth in any place where he sojourneth, let the men of his place help him with silver, and with gold, and with goods, and with beasts, beside the freewill offering for the house of God that is in Jerusalem. Then rose up the chief of the fathers of Judah and Benjamin, and the priests, and the Levites, with all them whose spirit God had raised, to go up to build the house of the LORD which is in Jerusalem."

—Ezra 1:4–5 KJV

Most of my life I have been a supporter of the ministry of others. From the time I was just a boy, I have given to missions, churches, and good causes. I have always enjoyed supporting those to whom God has given a special calling.

In the twilight of my career, I ran a ministry called Pinnacle Forum with a special calling to help set Christ as the center of our culture. I was dependent on others to strengthen our ability to achieve our mission. Each month as I reviewed the list of those who donated to the ministry of Pinnacle Forum, my heart was touched in a special way, and I understood how the gifts of others strengthen the hands of those in ministry.

The walls of Jerusalem would have never been rebuilt without the help of those who gave. We will not be able to rebuild the spiritual foundation of our culture without much help and support of others. This Scripture has a whole new meaning for me. My prayer is that God will bless and prosper those who give to support this ministry. My heart is full of gratitude to those who strengthen the hands of others.

Whose hands can you strengthen today?

Jesus Declares His Mission

"Then He closed the book, and gave it back to the attendant and sat down. And the eyes of all who were in the synagogue were fixed on Him."

—Luke 4:20

Jesus was in the habit of going to the synagogue every Sabbath. This time, he stood to read and was handed the book of the prophet Isaiah. He read: "The spirit of the LORD is upon me, because He has anointed me to preach the gospel to the poor." To many people, the poor had no value, but they were important to Jesus.

"He has sent me to heal the brokenhearted, and to preach deliverance to the captive . . ." Many people have been and are captives to habits that bind them, as well as literally in physical captivity.

"And recovery of sight to the blind." The blind includes not only those physically blind, but also in darkness mentally and spiritually.

"To set at liberty those who are oppressed . . ." Jesus came to bring freedom and peace.

When Jesus finished, he returned the book and sat. Everyone's eyes were upon Him.

I have given over 2,500 speeches in all types of venues and places. When I have finished, I have never had every eye fixed on me. Usually they have had a look of relief on their faces. To have every eye upon Him, He had to have read the Scripture with an authority that communicated at a level they had not experienced before.

They heard Jesus tell them He was the Son of God, the fulfillment of the prophecy of Isaiah. They were all stunned. Their reactions were mixed, based on their backgrounds.

Jesus is still speaking to us today. He speaks to our hearts and says, "I am He who came to give you eternal life." Are you hearing Him? How are you responding to the good news?

THE FIRST COMMANDMENT

"Then God blessed them, and God said to them, 'Be fruitful and multiply, fill the earth and subdue it; have dominion over the fish of the sea, over the birds of the air, and over every living thing that moves on the earth.'"

—Genesis 1:28

God's first command was to be fruitful and multiply, to take charge over His creation. Not only did God give this commandment, He designed man in such a way that the greatest joys we experience are when we are living in harmony with His plan. The joy we experience at the birth of our children and grandchildren. The joys of watching them grow and develop. The joys of tasks accomplished. Watching the seeds you sow in life grow and produce results is a blessing born of obedience to His command. We are hard wired for growth and productivity.

The most miserable people we meet in life are those with no goals and no grand vision to inspire them to greater achievement.

One of the traps we must avoid as we accomplish our goals is to feel we have done all there is to be done. There is a monument to a climber in the Swiss Alps that simply says, "He died climbing." May that be true of all of us.

Stay faithful and keep multiplying!

SPEAK TO ME, GOD!

"Now the word of the LORD came to Jonah the son of Amittai, saying, 'Arise, go to Nineveh, that great city and cry out against it; for their wickedness has come up before Me.'"

—Jonah 1:1–2

Dear God, would you please speak to me today? I want to hear and know Your voice. Too often it seems I am just plunging through my day, trying to do my best, but hearing nothing from You. I would like to do better than that. God, I long to be Your man: to be someone You trust enough to communicate with.

You have spoken to me in the past. I have heard Your voice. Sometimes it is strong and clear, and I know You have spoken. Other times Your voice seems so faint and hard to understand. So many times I don't know what to do about situations and relationships in my life. I need Your guidance and help. What action should I take? Where should I go? What should I say?

Lord, You know I don't listen well to others. Could You help me learn to be a better listener? Help me understand what others are trying to tell me. Most of all, Lord, teach me to listen to You.

Jonah heard Your voice, and he did not obey You. You had to teach him a great lesson. If I obey what You tell me to do, will You speak to me more often?

Forgive me for the times I have not acted on what You told me to do. Create a new spirit in my heart that listens better and seeks to obey. Let me do it today!

THE STIRRING OF HEARTS

"Now in the first year of Cyrus king of Persia, that the word of the LORD by the mouth of Jeremiah might be fulfilled, the LORD stirred up the spirit of Cyrus king of Persia, so that he made a proclamation throughout all his kingdom, and also put it in writing saying, 'Thus says Cyrus king of Persia: All the kingdoms of the earth the LORD God of heaven has given me. And He has commanded me to build Him a house at Jerusalem which is in Judea.'"

—Ezra 1:1–2

The Bible says that the Spirit stirred the heart of Cyrus, king of Persia, to call the Jews to go to Jerusalem and build a temple for Him. This is amazing! Why would a pagan king in Babylon even know or care about a temple to a God that was not his own? The Jews were dispersed throughout his kingdom—a small sect among many.

God can stir the heart of anyone. He will see that His will is done, and He uses the rulers of the kingdoms of the world to accomplish His purpose.

For many years Babylon was influenced by a godly leader named Daniel. Kings had come and gone, yet Daniel prospered under them all. When Cyrus became king, it is likely he sought out the counsel of Daniel, who by then would have been an old man with incredible social capital. He was in a position to instruct Cyrus on what God wanted him to do. Daniel was going about doing the Lord's will while Cyrus was running his kingdom; and all the while, God was bringing them together to accomplish His purpose.

God still stirs the hearts of leaders today. God is building leaders who will influence kings and shape kingdoms. Be excellent in your calling, and you will be surprised how God will use you. God still stirs the hearts of leaders today!

THE MIGHTY HAVE FALLEN

"The king spoke, saying, 'Is not this great Babylon, that I have built for a royal dwelling by my mighty power and for the honor of my majesty?' While the word was still in the king's mouth, a voice fell from heaven, 'King Nebuchadnezzar, to you it is spoken: the kingdom has departed from you!'"

—Daniel 4:30–31

One of the themes found throughout the Bible is that being a mighty person is a temporary condition. Leaders of all types and descriptions are faced sooner or later with laying down the scepter of power. How we do that is often determined by the condition of our heart. King Nebuchadnezzar had many accomplishments in his life. Rather than acknowledging the blessing of God and the role of the many who had helped him create these achievements, he said, "I did it. Look how wonderful I am." The next thing he knew, he was out in the field grazing with the sheep. The mighty had fallen.

If we begin to believe in our own magnificence and discover we are full of pride, we should fall to our knees and repent before God. If not, our circumstances in life may be changed and not in ways we would hope. Because of God's love for us, He will discipline us as He did Nebuchadnezzar.

The good news is that Nebuchadnezzar did repent and acknowledge that God was the one who had blessed him, and his sanity and his kingdom were restored.

We need to thank God today for His blessing and walk in a humble spirit.

WHAT DETERMINES OUR WALK

"If we live in the Spirit, let us also walk in the Spirit."
—Galatians 5:25

As a young man, I went for a period of about one year without a car. Cars were always important to me, and I owned a car before I could drive. I had made the mistake of trading a paid-for car for a newer car with a payment book. It was a nice car, but it was more car than I could afford. I then took a new job with a low salary in a new city. It looked like a job I would enjoy with good potential, but it just did not pay well.

I visited a friend who looked over my budget and told me I could not afford a car on what I was making. He suggested I get rid of the car. I did so and spent the next year of my life doing a lot of walking. I walked to work, I walked to church, and I walked to the bus lines. I walked everywhere.

Here are some of the things I learned about walking:

You need to know where you want to go.

It always helps to set a steady pace.

You should stay alert for changing conditions.

Walking in the Spirit is much the same. We know when we walk with Jesus, our destination is to become what He is calling us to be. We also know that consistent steady walking is much better than sprints and periods of inactivity. We need to always be alert for changes in our situations in life. We have an enemy who would like to send us on detours if we let him.

When we walk with God in His spirit, we will enjoy love, joy, long-suffering, peace, goodness, faith, meekness, and self-control. Sounds like a good way to walk, don't you think?

KEY TO SUCCESS

"Therefore David inquired of the LORD saying, 'Shall I go and attack these Philistines?'"

—1 Samuel 23:2

I saw a commercial on TV this week promoting a book entitled, *The Law of Success*. It made me think of the many books I have read and courses I have taken on how to become successful. After many years of study, I have come to the conclusion that you can't beat turning to the Bible as a resource for principles on this very subject. There is much we can learn about success from the first two kings of Israel, Saul and David.

Examining the patterns in their lives, you notice one major difference between the two men. Saul had a pattern of deciding what he was going to do and then asking God to bless it. David had a pattern of first asking God what he should do and then doing it.

I have to ask myself which of these men I am most often like. I am not sure I like the answer to the question, but I have a clear idea of which one I should be like.

I pray God will help me today to seek His will and direction in my life and think more about doing His will and less about my own plans.

GOT MONEY?

"For the love of money is the root of all kinds of evil."
—2 Timothy 6:10

Throughout my life, I have enjoyed making money. As a boy I spend many hours on my knees pulling dandelions out of my neighbor's lawn for a few dimes and quarters. I sold produce, mowed lawns, and delivered papers for meager wages. But I enjoyed it—at least the getting paid part.

As I got older, I started to set financial goals. When I achieved them, I would set higher goals. I loved to make money and have money, but I don't feel like I have ever had a love of money.

You are a lover of money if you'll do anything to get it, and you are unwilling to give money away. I have never felt that way. I have enjoyed having money to be able to give it away. I love to give money to my church and worthwhile organizations which do good things with the money. I love to give to the needs of my family.

I talked to a very wealthy businessman once who said, "I have had a lot of money in my life, but the money has never had me."

What are your attitudes and thoughts about money? Do you enjoy being a producer and a giver of money?

FACING ADVERSITY

"Then the people of the land tried to discourage the people of Judah. They troubled them in building, and hired counselors against them to frustrate their purpose all the days of Cyrus king of Persia, even until the reign of Darius king of Persia."

—Ezra 4:4–5

One thing we can always count on when we set out to follow God's call in our life is that we will suffer adversity.

It would seem that God, being all-powerful, would give us a smooth path to our goal or purpose. Instead, He is more inclined to allow adversity and obstacles into our lives. In this passage of Scripture, we see that all the people of Judah and Benjamin who returned to Jerusalem to rebuild the house of God encountered all kinds of frustration getting the work done.

As we study the patterns of how God works, we begin to realize that He is in the business of building character and directing us to become like Christ. Sometimes it takes adversity to build character that honors God and serves His purpose.

When I was a young man, a friend introduced me to the world of weightlifting. I soon learned the way to get stronger is to do more repetitions with heavier weights. I have noticed this principle exists in all of life. Heavy burdens and responsibilities build your capacity to do greater things.

As you follow God's call, you need to plan on adversity and obstacles coming your way. Then, when they occur, you can thank God for them, because you know He is building character and strength in you.

In the end, the task will be accomplished, and you will be on the way to becoming the person God intended you to be. Adversity is a blessing.

Is Your Walk Blameless?

"For the LORD God is a sun and shield; the LORD will give grace and glory; No good thing will he withhold from those who walk uprightly. O LORD of hosts, blessed is the man who trusts in You!"
—Psalm 84:11–12

It is human nature to desire honor and blessings. It is especially good when the blessings come from the Creator of the universe.

I have watched people who have worked diligently to exalt themselves. They have hired public relations experts to boost their image. They have hired and advanced people who fed their egos. They have become characters rather than people who desire character. Many times, their self-made image unravels, and the great story they have constructed about themselves and their greatness turns to rubbish.

God offers us a much better option. "I am Almighty God; walk before Me and be blameless" (Gen. 17:1). Do what is right, because it is right. Become a person of character. Keep your word. Seek to know and do the will of God. Live with humility and a grateful heart. Think more of others and a bit less about yourself. Be a giver and develop a generous spirit. Welcome reproof and instruction. Seek to serve rather than to be served. Study God's plan for the world and get in harmony with it!

If we do these things, God will bless us in a way and in a time that will produce peace and joy in our lives.

THE IMAGE OF GOD

"So God created man in His own image, in the image of God He created him, male and female He created them."

—Genesis 1:27

The entire Christian worldview should be based on the concept that we are created in the image of God. An image is a reflection of the real thing.

My sister just had a new grandson. As I looked at the picture of the new baby, I could see a reflection of my sister. He is a cute boy, and if he continues to reflect his grandmother, he will most likely be smart and a bit mischievous.

All of us are designed to reflect the image of God. A reflection is not the real thing. We are not God! We are not the center of the universe. I have seen some folks who adopt that worldview, becoming absorbed in self, thinking their words and thoughts superior to others. If we are to be a reflection of God, we need to learn His attributes and strive to be like Him.

From this passage in Genesis, it is clear that God is our Creator. Having been created in His image, we have creative gifts that add beauty and pleasure to life. Who can deny the satisfaction of completing a task, a project, a good deed?

Today, look for ways you can reflect the image of God in your world.

WALKING HUMBLY

"Then King David went in and sat before the LORD; and he said: 'Who am I, O LORD God? And what is my house that You have brought me thus far?'"

—2 Samuel 7:18

David started out as a shepherd boy and became a king. One of the things that endeared David to God and to the millions who have read his stories is the fact that he never lost his humility and his dependence on God. Even though he was a king, he was always a shepherd boy in his heart.

When I was a young speaker, I attended a meeting of speakers who were mostly experienced professionals. One of the greats on the platform was sharing his life's journey and made this statement: "You are in real trouble if you start believing what you have on your brochure."

Recently I walked by an open locker of a younger man at my golf club. His locker door was plastered with photos, and I was surprised to see all the pictures were of him! Where were the photos of his wife and family,I wondered? It caused me to reflect on the pictures I surround myself with and, most of all, the ones I project on the screen inside my head.

Am I like David who acknowledged, "You have brought me this far!" or do I revel in the greatness of all I have achieved? Because David walked humbly before God and had deep appreciation for all He had done in his life, God honored him and lifted him up.

BE A DILIGENT WORKER

"So the workmen labored, and the work was completed by them; they
restored the house of God to its original condition and reinforced it."
—2 Chronicles 24:13

The value of diligent leaders in any organization cannot be overestimated. Diligent leaders get the job done on any project.

In this case, they were rebuilding the temple. They had a workforce made up of masons, carpenters, and workers in iron and bronze. They were leaders who were like general contractors. They studied the original blueprints, assembled the materials, and organized the labor.

They were so effective that they got the job done under budget. They returned the unused funds to the king who used the money to acquire articles for the services in the temple. Because they were diligent with what they were entrusted to do, they were highly regarded.

The question we need to ask ourselves is, "How diligent am I in the tasks God has given me? Do I give value and produce results with the assignments I am given?"

God has called each of us to be diligent in our work. When we produce high quality results, we increase in favor and influence. Diligence is what enables us to transform our culture. Diligent workers become influential leaders whom God uses.

THE HEART OF WISDOM

"Now, O LORD my God, You have made Your servant king instead of my father David; but I am a little child; I do not know how to go out or come in. And Your servant is in the midst of Your people whom You have chosen, a great people, too numerous to be numbered or counted. Therefore give to Your servant an understanding heart to judge Your people, that I may discern between good and evil. For who is able to judge this great people of Yours?"

—1 Kings 3:7–9

A few years ago, my children were graduating from school and making decisions about their future. As I watched and listened to them and their friends, I realized it was very difficult to make good decisions without the wisdom that comes from experience. So I wrote the book, *Eight Critical Lifetime Decisions.* Several publishers asked to review the manuscript, but they all turned it down. The publishers agreed there wasn't a market for my book. In other words, young adults don't think they need advice.

Solomon's view of advice was different. He recognized that he needed help and prayed for wisdom. God gave it to him. Throughout the Bible we see that when people turn to God and say, "I am dependent on you. Show me what to do," God honors their request and then leads and directs them.

In America, we celebrate independence. We teach, "Do it your way," and as a result, we have turned away from wisdom. The Bible instructs us to do it God's way. Let the God who made you, run you! When you do, life gets better!

Tomorrow Will Be a Great Day

"And God will wipe away every tear from their eyes; there shall be no more death, nor sorrow, nor crying. There shall be no more pain, for the former things have passed away."

—Revelation 21:4

There was a song I like that started out, "If I could make the world the way I want to, what a day tomorrow would be!" Well, I can't make the world the way I want to, but Jesus can, and He will.

I know people who would like to improve their lives, fix their pains, and ease their burdens. Jesus can do all of that.

I know people who have lost their way in life. They wander and struggle. Jesus can give them hope and direction.

I know people who have created immense turmoil and havoc in their lives, resulting in problems that seem irreversible. Jesus can fix them.

There is coming a great day! Be encouraged, my friend, and cling to the promise of Jesus. Tomorrow will be a great day for those who love and serve Him.

Do You Know a Holy Place?

"Hallowed be Your name."

—Luke 11:2

We are taught throughout the Bible that God is holy, and He has a Spirit that inhabits people and places. When we come to a place where God dwells, we can sense His Spirit.

When the Iron Curtain came down and the country of Russia opened to Western business people, I spent a lot of time teaching former communists and KGB agents how to become business owners and employees of western companies. It was a fascinating assignment and taught me a great deal.

One thing I experienced was the power of the Holy Spirit to dwell in a specific place.

I was given a tour of the Kremlin. There is a house that down through the centuries was the home of the Patriarch of the Russian Orthodox Church. In this home, the work of the church was carried out. It is now a museum and a repository of much of the history of the Russian people. On the top floor of the home are the private chambers of the Patriarch. Next to his bedroom is a private prayer chapel where, through the years, the Patriarch would go to pray. When I walked through the curtains into the room, I could sense the Spirit of God. It was an awesome feeling.

Do you have a place where you go to commune with God? A specific place where you can sense the Spirit of God? Wherever we pray, we create a connection with a holy God, a place where we can sense His Spirit.

Do Not Despair

"When Joseph had taken the body, he wrapped it in a clean linen cloth, and laid it in his new tomb which he had hewn out of the rock; and he rolled a large stone against the door of the tomb, and departed."

—Matthew 27:59–60

It was a chilly, blustery day in April when I stood looking at my father's casket. I felt lost. Alone. Empty. I was seventeen years old and certainly not ready to say goodbye to my father.

That sorrowful day in my life helps me understand how the disciples felt when Jesus was laid in a tomb. They had spent the last few years of their lives following Jesus from city to city. They saw Him open blind eyes, raise the dead, and heal the lame and wounded in body and spirit. They had watched Him debate the nation's greatest scholars. They had seen Him love and care for children. He had taught them and loved them. Now, He was gone.

When you see your dreams die, life is hard to bear. When you feel lost and your heart is troubled, remember how Jesus spoke to His disciples, telling them not to be afraid and troubled. Because He rose from the dead, we are not without hope. We know that one day we will have the tears wiped from our eyes, and we will live in a land of no pain or sorrow.

Dear friends, keep your eyes on Jesus. There are good days coming!

Do You Have a Hard Heart?

"And Pharaoh's heart grew hard, and he did not heed them, as the Lord had said."

—Exodus 7:13

One of my fears in life is that I would develop a hard heart. Socrates once said, "The unexamined life is not worth living." Today I am doing a bit of a heart examination. I hope you still spend a bit of time with me thinking about this question: Do I have a hard heart?

I love to be with my grandchildren. One of the many reasons I enjoy them is they have such tender hearts. They are sweet and kind and loving. I just wish I could protect and shelter them from the world so that they could stay that way.

They make me wonder if I was ever that way. Was there a time in my life when I was tender and kind? I sort of remember being more like that a long, long time ago. I am still a little bit that way, but too often I let my heart harden. I have learned to shut people out and not listen to them. I have developed an ability to harden my heart toward people I should be more loving toward. Too often I am deaf to others' pleas and blind to their needs. I know my heart needs some softening.

Oh, great God who created me and this universe, please help me to see the world around me with the eyes of Jesus. Give me a heart that is kind and tender. I want to be more loving and trusting and obedient to Your will. Take the judgmental harshness out of my heart. Help me find someone today I can encourage and help lift their burden. Amen.

THE PROMISE OF RESTORATION

"So I will restore to you the years that the swarming locust has eaten . . ."

—Joel 2:25

Restoration is one of the great themes of the Bible. God continually reminds us that no matter how desperate the situation, restoration is possible. It is not guaranteed, but it is one option.

One of the other facts is the locusts. Those of us who live in cities don't fully appreciate the menace of locusts. They come in swarms and waves; they devour all vegetation and leave the land parched and barren. Locusts bring devastation.

We can have locust invasions of many types in our lives; they can come without warning and leave us parched and barren. Yet God holds out to us the promise of restoration. He can and will restore the years that locusts have stolen. People are given second chances. There is a promise of a better life for those who are willing to humble themselves before God and repent from the cause of personal locusts.

If you are currently experiencing a locust invasion, reach out to God. Ask Him to show you His path, and then take it. Restoration is just a prayer away!

PRAYING ALL NIGHT

"Now it came to pass in those days that He went out to the mountain
to pray, and continued all night in prayer to God."

—Luke 6:12

Jesus was a man of prayer. If we are going to emulate His life, we need
to pray. When Jesus faced critical points in His ministry, He often
spent the night in prayer to prepare Himself.

In this case, He was preparing to choose the disciples. These would
be the men He was counting on to carry His message to the world after
His death. He had three years to train and develop them. This was a
crucial time. He needed a clear mind and the ability to discern whom
God had chosen as His disciples. (I think He prayed because He knew
what they would eventually face.)

Have you ever found yourself facing moments in your life when
you need to make important decisions such as hiring key employees?
Has your response been to spend a night in prayer seeking God's
direction in your hiring decisions? I have heard people say, "I feel it is
God's will that I take this job." Until now, I have never thought to ask,
"How do you know that?" How much prayer went into the decision?
The even bigger question is, "Am I spending enough time in prayer to
discern the will of God?"

Unfortunately, I know the answer to that question. I am not praying enough. I need to find a way to make prayer a bigger priority in
my life.

How about you, my friend? Is seeking God's will in prayer a priority in your life? Are you in the midst of making an important decision?
How about trying an all-nighter?

THE BANNER OF THE CROSS

"But God forbid that I should boast except in the cross of our Lord Jesus Christ . . ."

—Galatians 6:14

Constantine was religious. As a pagan ruler, he worshipped many gods. He knew about Christ's death on the cross and had seen many Christians die for their faith in a similar manner. They died because they refused to worship the Roman emperors and their many other gods and goddesses.

In AD 312, Constantine was about to engage in a battle with a challenger to his position of emperor of the Western Roman Empire. Constantine's troops were greatly outnumbered. He faced what looked like certain defeat. The night before the battle, he saw a vision of the cross and had his soldiers adorn their shields with this holy symbol of sacrifice. Under the banner of the cross, they won the battle of Milvian Bridge. Constantine became the emperor and a great Christian leader. He ended the persecution of Christians and changed the history of western civilization.

Are you flying the banner of the cross? Do you work in Jesus' name? The goal of Pinnacle Forum and C-3 is to raise leaders who lead under the banner of the cross. We are to do mighty acts of service, win battles, and take the high ground under the banner of the cross.

God's Will Be Done

"Let the work of this house of God alone; let the governor of the Jews and the elders of the Jews build this house of God on its site. Moreover, I issue a decree as to what you shall do for the elders of these Jews, for the building of this house of God: Let the cost be paid at the king's expense from taxes on the region beyond the River; this is to be given immediately to these men, so that they are not hindered."

—Ezra 6:7–8

When God told the Jews to go back to Jerusalem and rebuild the temple, they got permission from King Cyrus. When they started to build, they encountered opposition from the local people who appealed to a new king, Artaxerxes, to stop the building. He ordered it stopped. Then, Darius became king of Persia. When the Jews appealed to Darius, he researched Cyrus's decree to build the temple and permitted the Jews to move forward.

Rest assured, what God wants to happen will come to pass. When God gives us a calling, we must believe the work will get done. Despite opposition, struggles, and difficult times, God will help us to achieve His objectives.

One of the interesting parts of this story in Ezra is how the leaders who opposed rebuilding the temple eventually helped pay for its construction. It is not a good idea to oppose the will of God. King Darius ordered those who were in violation of his order to have timber pulled down from their houses and have them impaled on it. This decree resulted in great cooperation from the former enemies of the Jews. Soon, the temple was built.

It's a good idea to be on God's side!

THE MIRACLE OF MULTIPLICATION

"Then a man came from Baal Shalisha, and brought the man of God bread of the firstfruits, twenty loaves of barley bread and newly ripened grain in his knapsack. And he said, 'Give it to the people, that they may eat.' And his servant said, 'What? Shall I set this before one hundred men?' He said again, 'Give it to the people, that they may eat; for thus says the LORD, They shall eat and have some left over.'"

—2 Kings 4:42–43

God is in the business of multiplication. He takes the gifts we bring to Him and multiplies them.

In this story, a man brings the firstfruits of tithes to the prophet. They consisted of twenty loaves of barley bread. Elisha was entertaining a crowd of one hundred men, and he told the servant to feed the crowd with that gift of bread. The servant said, "No way. There is not enough to feed them." Elisha said to do it anyway. The servant complied, and after they had eaten, there was still some left.

When we are faithful in bringing our first fruits to God, He has a way of multiplying them for His purpose. God multiplies our gifts so they accomplish more than we could imagine. God loves faithful people. Can you imagine the joy of the faithful man who brought his gift and saw God multiply it?

What gifts are you bringing to God? Your talents? Your time? Your money? When you give, you open a storehouse of matching gifts that exceeds anything you could imagine.

Get in harmony with God's plan of multiplication today.

Partners in the Gospel

"I thank my God upon every remembrance of you, always in every prayer of mine for you all making request with joy, for your fellowship in the gospel from the first day until now; being confident of this very thing, that He which hath begun a good work in you will perform it until the day of Jesus Christ: just as it is right for me to think this of you all, because I have you in my heart; in as much as both in my bonds, and in the defense and confirmation of the gospel, ye all are partakers of my grace."

—Philippians 1:3–7

It is a wonderful thing to be a partner. I have never felt quite worthy to be a partner of Pinnacle Forum, and I am thankful I was accepted. It is a privilege. I feel the same way about my relationship to God. Never have I been worthy to be a partner in the family of God, but I am so grateful to be a part of it.

We talk about being personally transformed as partners in God's family. The Scripture talks about how God will continue to improve or transform us until the day of Jesus Christ. It sounds like God has a big job on His hands.

We need to constantly be reproved and approved. If we think of ourselves as partners, we should let God reprove us, and we can approve each other.

I am thankful for all my partners in God's work. I pray that God will bless you, that He will guide you, and that He will grow you into the likeness of His image. These verses are my prayer for you. It's great to be partners with you and God!

How's Your Social Capital?

"A good name is to be chosen rather than great riches, loving favor rather than silver or gold."

—Proverbs 22:1

I was visiting a friend who was a CPA in a medium-sized city. We had a mutual acquaintance who was a real estate developer, and I asked him how the man was doing.

"Not too well," he replied. "He's run out of social capital."

"What do you mean by that?" I asked.

He explained, "He burned everyone in town he's done business with, and now no one wants to work with him."

When I was on the senior loan committee of Sherwood and Roberts, I noticed one developer we worked with always seemed to get better terms than anyone else. I asked my boss about that, and he said, "We have worked with him for a long time, and we know he will always keep his commitments."

It makes a big difference in your life if you focus on building social capital. Keep your commitments. Do what you say you will do. Always leave something in the deal for the other guy. Be considerate of others and easy to do business with. Do what is right. Extend a hand up to others. Speak well of others.

Build your social capital, and financial capital won't be far behind.

How is your social capital account?

Ready for Some Coaching?

"Search me, O God, and know my heart; Try me, and know my anxieties; And see if there is any wicked way in me, and lead me in the way everlasting."

—Psalm 139:23–24

I am developing a whole new perspective on the subject of coaching. I take my grandson to a baseball training facility where they really know how to coach baseball. They watch his swing mechanics and show him how to improve. The result is, he keeps getting better at baseball.

Coaching is not limited, however, to the world of sports. Coaching for success takes place in all areas, including business.

Jessica was a very young woman when she purchased her Express Employment Professionals franchise. Her coach and trainer, Tammy, was experienced and wise—a great trainer. It was a joy to watch Tammy coach and mentor Jessica's professional growth and success in building an outstanding business. Good coaching builds championship performance.

God wants to be your life coach. He will guide and direct you and help you avoid mistakes and become all He created you to be. Are you allowing Him to be your coach?

God Calling

"Then the boy Samuel ministered to the LORD before Eli. And the word of the LORD was rare in those days. There was no widespread revelation."

—1 Samuel 3:1

"Then the LORD came and stood and called as at other times: 'Samuel! Samuel!' And Samuel answered, 'Speak, for your servant hears.'"

—1 Samuel 3:10

It is always amazing to me how God can change the destiny of a people through one dedicated servant. Samuel listened and obeyed God, and God changed Israel.

William Wilberforce was called by God to fight the evil of the slave trade in England. He organized opposition and worked consistently until parliament passed a bill on February 23, 1807 to abolish the slave trade. Wilberforce was a devout Christian and organized many social groups that helped the poor. He worked to rouse the moral conscience of a nation. He brought the values of Jesus to the people of England.

God can do great things through people who listen and do His will. What does God want to do through you? Listen to God's call as Samuel and Wilberforce did, and God will amaze you.

Are You Hopeful?

"Now may the God of hope fill you with all joy and peace in believing, that you may abound in hope by the power of the Holy Spirit."
—Romans 15:13

Hope is one of the most important parts of life. To be a hopeful person is to be a happy, optimistic person.

Victor Frankl in his great book *Man's Search for Meaning* tells of his experience in a Nazi concentration camp in World War II. He tells of a prisoner who had a dream that the allies were going to come and free them in July. They didn't come. He had been in a great place emotionally when he felt they were coming. After they failed to come, he lost all hope, crawled in his bed, and died.

Frankl's conclusion was that as long as people had hope they could survive any indignity they were subjected to. When hope died, they died too.

God is our source of hope. He fills us with His joy and peace. His promises give us hope for each day. When we know He is in control, we have hope. He tells us all things will produce goodness in our lives.

We also have the hope of eternal life. Whatever happens in this life, when it is over, we will have a wonderful future.

Where are you placing your hope, my friend?

GRACE TO YOU!

"So as sin reigned in death, even so grace might reign through righteousness to eternal life through Jesus Christ our Lord."
—Romans 5:21

A good friend of mine recently told me his favorite word lately was *grace*. He caused me to think more about grace. When I think of grace, two things come to my mind: one is forgiveness, the other is acceptance.

Jesus Christ died to provide forgiveness for our sins and give us eternal life. Because we are forgiven, we should forgive others. It is great to be forgiven and to forgive others.

The second thing grace made me think about is acceptance of others. God sees us not as we are, but as we can become. We need to look at others the same way.

We need to give grace to others by seeing the good in them. Everyone has areas of their life where they need improvement. Grace is overlooking the negative things and focusing on the positive aspects in each person.

May God fill you with His grace.

GOD AND NATIONS

"If My people who are called by My name will humble themselves, and pray and seek My face and turn from their wicked ways, I will hear from heaven and will forgive them their sin and will heal their land."

—2 Chronicles 7:14

I was flying back from Russia. The Iron Curtain had recently come down, and I was on an assignment to help teach former communists how to work with Western companies. It had been a fascinating week. I came home more convinced than ever that free market economies work wonderfully well and government controlled economies are a disaster.

I was sitting next to the Russian ambassador to the UN. She asked me what I thought of her country. I responded that I loved the people, and I felt the country had great potential. I told her how I loved seeing all the beautiful Russian churches, and I was amazed at the long lines of people waiting to get into the church.

She said, "We made a great mistake in not letting our people go to church. I have two boys who have started to go to church, and they are becoming better boys."

I don't know what the future holds for Russia, but I believe if they allow their people to go to church and worship God, their nation will grow and prosper.

I wonder what will happen to America if we continue to persecute and discriminate against Christians with Bible-based beliefs. We need a revival in our country.

DESIGNED TO CLIMB

"A good man out of the good treasure of his heart brings forth good."
—Luke 6:45

For several years I have been urging people to find the high ground in their life. The high ground is the place on one of the seven mountains of culture: family, business, media, education, arts and entertainment, religion, and government. On these peaks, you can use your personal influence to help shape the culture in a way that pleases God.

You are a unique creation of God. You were created with a purpose. When I was a young man, I wrote out a purpose statement for my life. It was: "My purpose is to develop my talents and abilities to their fullest and use them to serve others." As I have grown and developed over the years, I have come to know and use my abilities to do that.

Looking back, I can see how God had a wonderful plan for my life. He has used me to serve others, and as I am coming to the end of my journey, I can see how God's plan was a good one for me.

What gifts has God given you? How are you using those gifts to impact our culture in a positive way? Find some high ground for your life and do some climbing!

WHERE ARE YOUR SINS?

"You will cast all our sins into the depths of the sea."

—Micah 7:19

I looked into a crystal-clear pool of water. It was beautiful. Fish swam in the sparkling water, and the sun cast shadows on the rocks in the bottom. No blemish clouded the pool. My sins were not there.

Another day I stood on the deck of a great ship and looked at the water below us. It was dark and deep. Nothing was visible below the surface. That's where my sins were buried. Because of Jesus' death on the cross, my sins are buried in the deepest sea.

I'm so glad Jesus loved me enough to die and forgive my sins. I am freed from the guilt of yesterday. When I stand before God's throne, I can say my sins are covered by Jesus' blood and have been buried in the deepest sea.

My friend, are your sins in the crystal pool or in the darkest sea?

KEEP PRAYING!

I was in college and stopped by my pastor's home to visit. As we were chatting, a knock came at the front door. The pastor opened the door, and there stood a large, gruff man. He was sobbing. "I'm going to take this fellow next door to the church," the pastor said to me. "Want to come?"

As soon as we entered the church, we went straight to the altar and began to pray. The pastor would pray. The man would pray. I would pray. Then, we would start all over again.

I later learned the man we were praying for was from California, he had a drinking problem, and he had lost his wife and family. He recently moved to Nampa, Idaho, to stay with his aunt. He was a broken-hearted man in desperate need.

We kept praying. There was a great spirit of oppression, and it seemed that in spite of our prayers, God wasn't showing up. Finally, after two hours of earnest prayer, God came! The Holy Spirit came down and turned a broken sinner into a man of God. He was delivered, forgiven, and filled with new motivation and purpose. Real victory often only comes after much travail.

While we were praying, God gave me a vision of what He had in store for this man's future. His name was Earl, and I perceived that he would become a pillar in the church and would marry my widowed mother. Sure enough, he became my stepfather.

Do you need a miracle in your life? Keep praying. God is standing near, waiting to answer.

WHAT A DAY!

"Then I, John, saw the holy city, New Jerusalem coming down out of heaven from God, prepared as a bride adorned for her husband. And I heard a loud voice from heaven saying, 'Behold the tabernacle of God is with men, and He shall dwell with them, and they shall be His people. God Himself will be with them and be their God. And God will wipe away every tear from their eyes; there shall be no more pain.'"

—Revelation 21:2–4

If I could make the world the way I wanted, what a day tomorrow would be. There would be no children without parents to love and care for them.

There would be no pain and suffering. The lame could walk, and the blind could see.

There would be no hatred and bloodshed between people. There would be everlasting peace.

All people would be free to grow and develop their talents.

Relationships would last forever.

It sounds like we would all be in heaven. I plan to go and hope to see you there!

Finding Your Sweet Spot

All great achievement in life is the result of a person finding and using the sweet spot in their unique design. Your sweet spot is where you connect the gifts, talents, and abilities God has given you with a great passion.

You can find your sweet spot by listing all the gifts and talents you have. Also list the skills you have been given. Then, make a list of all the things you are passionate about. Your passions come from the beliefs and desires of your heart. Ask yourself, "If I could change my world, what would it look like?" or "If I could accomplish one thing before I die, what would that be?" or "How could I use my gifts and abilities to enrich the lives of others?"

My friend Norm Hagen was gifted with analytical skills, common sense, and an ability to get along with and encourage others. He studied accounting in college and found his sweet spot in building two very successful accounting practices.

In his retirement years, he loves to serve the homeless in Seattle by running a rescue van program through his church. The van takes meals to the homeless in Seattle on Friday nights.

Have you found your sweet spot?

THE VIEW FROM MY CHAIR

My home has a beautiful view of the Puget Sound and the Olympic Mountains. The chair I normally sit in has my back to the view. I have to make a conscious effort to turn around and see the view. When I do that, it is worth the effort.

This principle applies to people as well. When I am so focused on myself, I miss the beauty of other people. To see the beauty in others, I need to get my eyes off myself and learn more about those around me.

A speaker was driving home from a speaking engagement. He had been jabbering away to his wife, and all of a sudden, he realized all he had been talking about was himself. He was checked in his spirit because his wife was so quiet, so he said, "I'm sorry. I've just been talking about myself. Let's talk about you. How did you like my speech?"

Turn around and discover the beauty of the people around you. Get them to talk about their hopes, dreams, and ambitions. You'll enjoy the view.

Six Essentials for Teachers and Preachers

1. Teach 100 percent surrender to God's will.
2. Be filled with and be led by the Holy Spirit.
3. Live a holy lifestyle.
4. Be thrifty. Be a consistent giver and saver.
5. Be a lifetime learner, always growing and getting better.
6. Live in harmony with all people.

CONSIDER THE OPTIONS

A dog food company was having a meeting of their salespeople. The president of the company scolded his team: "We need to sell more dog food!"

One little salesman in the back row finally stood up and said, "The problem is the dogs. They don't like it."

The company should have focused on making a better product instead of beating up on the sales team.

When you face a problem in your business, one of the keys to solving it is to think realistically and thoroughly. Instead of placing blame, get outside the box and think of all the options.

If you are stuck, get help. A good place to start is with your employees. Ask them for their opinions. Their opinions may be different from yours and often times are very valuable. If they are not willing to talk to you, bring in a consultant to help you. I did this many times with clients and helped move the company forward.

Good thinking leads to good results.

ON RECRUITING

When I was a professional recruiter, I interviewed many people. Trying to evaluate them was always a challenge. One thing I tried to find out was if a candidate had ten years of experience or one year of experience, ten times.

I would ask questions such as: What do you read, when do you read, and why do you read? What have you been doing to get better at what you do? What have you learned about your job that you didn't know when you took it? What is your goal for self-improvement?

The patterns in people's lives will help you predict their future. Hire people whom you can help grow and improve, and your business will grow and get better.

The story is told of the man who got a note with his paycheck. "You are about to receive a substantial raise. It will become effective when you do."

PRODUCTIVITY

Some employees are not as productive as you would like them to be. How you analyze and deal with them is a key aspect of being a great leader. A little tool I have used effectively can help you develop a plan to work with each person individually.

Rate them on a scale of one to ten in their attitude and in their skills, ten being the highest rating and one being the lowest. Attitude is how they feel about their job, their company, and their work. Give them the same rating on the skills they have to do the job. Then use the following chart to build a plan of review:

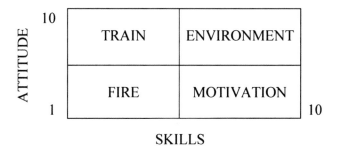

If they are high in attitude and low in skills, get them training.

If they are low in attitude and high in skills, get them motivated. Maybe they need incentives. Maybe you need to rearrange their job to give them more challenges.

If they are high in attitude and skills, you have an environmental problem. It could be something internal: job structure, relationship skills, or tools. It might be something external such as a personal problem. Find out and help solve the problem.

If they are low in both attitude and skills, fire them and release them to go elsewhere.

If you follow these suggestions, your productivity will increase.

LESSONS ABOUT LIFE FROM BASEBALL

I am spending the weekend watching a baseball tournament for thirteen-year-olds. As I have observed and listened, I have noticed some wonderful parallels between baseball and the business of selling. I would like to share them with you in hopes you will find them encouraging and helpful.

Did you get a hit? One of the questions that baseball players and sales people are most frequently asked is, "Did you get a hit?" or in sales speak, "Did you make a sale?" This is a great question to answer if you just got a hit or a sale; however, it's not much fun if you struck out or didn't get up to bat.

Many factors influence whether we get hits or make sales. Let's examine them to see if we can learn some lessons applying to baseball and to sales.

You cannot control results! If you could control results, all batters would hit 1000 percent, and all sales people would never lose a sale. Neither baseball nor sales are that easy. You cannot control whether you hit or not, but there are factors you can control. Spend more time on the 90 percent of hitting you can control, and the 10 percent you cannot control will produce better results.

Let's think for a bit on the aspects you can control.

You can control your attitude. You cannot control a lot of things that happen to you, but you can control your responses to them. Always keep your head high. Nothing looks worse than a player who misses a ball or strikes out and hangs their head and slowly walks to the dugout looking like someone just ran over their puppy. Always keep your head up and hustle. Sales people and baseball players can always project a positive and enthusiastic attitude.

Learn from your failures! There is always a reason why we experience failures. We need to try to understand and correct those. Baseball players all have "holes" in their bats: spots where they are most likely to miss a pitch. Fast balls. Curve balls. Change-ups. High pitches. Low pitches. Pitches inside or outside. Somewhere, there is an area they tend to miss the pitch. Sales people also find there are some sales they miss more often. It is also true that some pitches and zones over the plate are easier for a hitter to succeed in. A good hitter will know that area of the plate and look for his pitch. Sales people too have certain types of companies and people they are more effective with.

The key to effectiveness as a salesman and a baseball player is to become a *meaningful specific* rather than a *wandering generality*. A wandering generality is someone who comes to the ballpark unprepared and without a plan. They go through the motions of being a player and giving it their best effort. A meaningful specific comes to the ballpark with a strategy based on research. They are prepared and ready to get results. Becoming a meaningful specific involves preparation.

Turn your weakness into strength. Hall of Fame baseball players and salesmen have learned to turn their weakness into strengths. Most players have a hard time hitting pitches on the outside of the plate. A great player will turn this weakness into strength. They could decide they will hit one hundred balls every day on the outside corner of the plate. This can be done by positioning a batting tee on the outside corner of the plate, adjusted to various heights, then hitting the ball with the goal of driving it to the opposite side of the field. This type of discipline will improve the ability to drive the outside pitch and increase effectiveness and confidence.

The same principle works for salespeople. Let's imagine a salesperson is getting a low percentage of orders for the number of appointments they have. Most likely this is caused by an ineffective sales presentation. This can be improved by taking one aspect of the sales presentation and working out a plan that uses practice and repetition.

Start with the questions you ask in a sales presentation. Write them out and practice saying them until they feel comfortable to say and thought provoking to hear. Practice and repetition will turn your weakness into strength.

Be a team player. All players have times of struggle. Things don't always work the way you would like them to. You cannot always control the outcome of your activities, but you can control your effort and attitude.

Encourage and support your teammates. Hustle, hustle, hustle. Clean up the dugout. Pick up and organize the bats. Show respect to the coaches and umpires. Be early. Take extra batting and fielding practice. Focus on others not yourself. Relax and work on smoother motions. Focus on details. Watch the seams on the baseball. A great attitude and a great effort will help raise the performance of your whole team.

Salespeople need to apply the same principles to their work. One day I was talking to a sales manager about one of his people who was struggling to make sales. The sales manager said, "I cannot get rid of him. Every morning he comes in early and makes the coffee for the office."

Never give up. Edgar Martinez grew up in Puerto Rico. The first year he played on a little league team, he went the entire year without getting a hit. His last game of the season he faced the best pitcher in the league. He hit a solid grounder to the shortstop but was thrown out at first base. He said at that moment, he knew he could become a good hitter.

He kept working at getting better. Eventually he was signed to a professional baseball contract by the Seattle Mariners. His first year, he had a batting average of .178. He kept working on getting better. Before he retired he was recognized as one of the greatest hitters to have ever played the game. He had a lifetime batting average of .313 and won four batting titles.

It pays to keep trying and getting better whether you are a baseball player or a salesman. Champions in sales and baseball are those who keep trying. The only time you are beaten is when you give up.

How to Build a Great Organization

What is your *vision*? What do you plan to do that will make the world a better place?

Express Employment Professionals started with a vision of creating a franchise network in the employment industry that gave franchise owners a team to belong to.

What is your *mission*? How will you fulfill the vision?

Express has a mission of helping people find good jobs and helping employers find good people.

What are your *founding principles/values*? These create your company culture.

Express started with the following values:

Express will be a sales and marketing-focused company.
Express will be committed to spiritual and family values.
Express will operate with integrity.
Express will help franchise owners and employers achieve their goals.
Express will value education and focus on training.
Express will be excellent at what we do.
Express will create opportunity for financial success.
Express will be a loyal organization.

What is your *goal*?

Express started with the following goal: To be the number one staffing company. To accomplish this goal, Express developed these *strategies*:

Have great, well-trained sales people in the field
Provide our sales team with tools and training

Have lots of sales team recognition
Provide education for staff
Provide systems that increase productivity
Help franchise owners sell and manage better

GOD'S UNIQUE PARTNERSHIP

"If you count me as a partner receive him as you would me. But if
he has wronged you or owes you anything, put that on my account."
—Philemon 1:17–18

I first began to learn about partnership when I was a young man. I was
in a town I had never been to before. I knew just one person who lived
there. He had a small professional business. I went and visited him.

He was all excited about a man he had recently met and formed a
partnership with. A couple of years later, I was in the town again and
once again went to visit my friend. Then I learned (as Paul Harvey used
to say), "the rest of the story."

It seems he and his partner had done very well in a building supply
company. Then one day he showed up for work and found that his
partner had embezzled the money from the company and left him with
all the bills. He became a broken man and never again achieved the
prominence he had once known.

Partnerships can be disastrous if you choose the wrong partner. On
the other hand, I have seen some great partnerships over the years.

I have two friends in the development business. One is a very
aggressive, hard-driving salesman. He loves to sell and make things
happen. His partner is a more conservative detail guy. He makes sure
that things are well thought out and looks after the fiscal side of the
business. Together they are more successful than either one of them
would be on their own.

Partnerships can be a wonderful experience if you have the right
partner.

I have thought about this a lot and wondered what I would like in
a partner. Here is what I would look for:

- I would like a partner with know-how. I learned a long time ago, if you are ever going to be in *Who's Who,* you first of all need to know what's what! If you don't know what's what, you are more likely to be in *Who's Through.*
- I would like a partner with lots of knowledge we could use in the partnership. I have traveled a lot in my lifetime and stayed in many hotels. I think I know how a great hotel should be operated. I have thought many times I should go into the hotel business. If I did, I would like to have Bill Marriott as my partner. He operates the Marriott Hotel chain. They really know how to run a great hotel. I would go to Mr. Marriott and say, "I want to be your partner in the hotel business. I'll work hard and do whatever you tell me to do." I'm sure if I could convince Bill Marriott to be my partner, I would be a great success in the hotel business.
- I have spent a lot of time in the real estate business, and I always enjoyed working in that field. If I wrote a business plan on how to build a great real estate company, the next thing I would need would be a partner with some resources. I would like to have Bill Gates as my partner. I would go to him and say, "Mr. Gates, let's be partners in the real estate business. Let's use my knowledge and expertise and your money, and we'll build a great business together." I'm sure if I could convince Bill Gates to be my partner, I'd soon be a great success in the real estate business.
- I would not only love to have a partner with knowledge and resources, but I would also like to have a partner who understands me. I don't know about you, but a great part of my life is spent wondering if anyone understands what I am trying to do. Having a partner who you are compatible with is a great asset.

I am here today to tell you that *God wants to be your partner.* Do you think He has the qualifications?

He is the source of all the knowledge you will ever need. Daniel 2:20–22 says: "Blessed be the name of God forever and ever, for wisdom and might are His, and He changes the times and the seasons. He removes kings and raises up kings. He gives wisdom to the wise and knowledge to those who have understanding. He reveals the deep and sacred things, and the light dwells in Him!" When you are partners with God, you have all the knowledge you need available to you. He created the world. He owns the world, and everything in it belongs to Him. When God is your partner, you have all the resources you will ever need.

God understands you. He created you and knows everything about you. He knows your thoughts, your desires, and your goals. He knows your strengths and weaknesses. He wants to grow and develop you. He wants to help you find and develop your mission. Most of all, He loves you enough to send his Son to die for you!

Do you think God would make a great partner?

The Christians I feel the sorriest for are those who limit themselves to their own resources, knowledge, and understanding. They are like the couple I heard about who always wanted to take a cruise. They saved up their money and bought a ticket on a luxurious cruise ship. By the time they got to the ship, they were running out of money, so they bought some cheese, crackers, snacks, and dried fruit to eat on board. Whenever dinner was being served, they went to their cabin and ate the provisions they had brought along.

Finally, the last night of the cruise, they decided to splurge. Making their way to the dining room, they timidly asked the porter, "How much will it cost us to have dinner here tonight."

The porter blinked in surprise. "There is no cost, sir. All food is included in the price of your ticket." They had been barely eating the whole trip when they could have been enjoying the finest food the world has to offer.

Too many Christians make that same mistake. They make their lives a subsistence diet, when God wants it to be a banquet.

Several years ago I was having coffee with a friend of mine named John. He was telling me about what a hard time he was having financially. I asked him, "John, I know you are a Christian; do you pay your tithe?"

"No," he replied. "I can't even pay my bills, let alone pay my tithe."

I said, "John, God wants to be your partner, and if you put Him in charge of your finances, I am sure He will help you."

He said, "Ralph, I'll do it."

One year later he told me, "All my bills are paid, and I bought a house I am going to rent out. God sure makes a great partner."

Down through the years, I have watched him grow and prosper. He has done very well.

How to Hire Good People

When I first started in the employment business, I was taught to evaluate job candidates on four criteria: appearance, personality, values, and logic. These ideas have served me well over the years and are still valuable in making hiring decisions.

Appearance is important, but the most changeable of the four qualities. How a candidate looks and packages himself/herself gives us a good idea of their self-image. Appearance can be easily changed with a little work, so it has value but needs to be interpreted correctly. I am often interested in someone's ability to change.

Personality is a key feature on many jobs. I look at personality to determine how people will fit in a specific work environment. Shy and quiet people may fit well in one job, but not another. Evaluate personality based on the needs of a job to make good matches.

Values are the key to people's behavior. If you know what people believe and value, you can understand what their actions will likely be. The more you learn about what people believe the more you can understand what they will do in a given situation. Learn all you can about a person's education, associates, and interests if you want to be able to predict their method of making choices.

Logic is a person's ability to distill wisdom from knowledge. An example would be someone whose income is $2,000 per month and expenses are $2,000 who borrows $200 extra per month to increase their standard of living. A person with logic would never do that because they know sooner or later they will have to pay the money back with interest. Being logical is making good decisions based on good information.

If you make hiring decisions based on these criteria, you might not always make the right decision, but you will tend to improve your percentage of good hires.

TAKING THE HIGH GROUND

On the first of July 1863, the Union and Confederate armies clashed in Gettysburg, Pennsylvania. Brigadier General Henry Hunt, chief of artillery of the Army of the Potomac, moved his guns to the top of Cemetery Hill. By 5:15 that afternoon, the Army of Northern Virginia mounted a full assault on the Confederate army. From the high ground of Cemetery Hill, Hunt's soldiers poured enough firepower into the Confederates to break their charge and win a decisive victory for the Union. The Union prevailed because they occupied the high ground.

Those holding the high ground in any battle are in a strong position to win. Enemies of the soul of America have for many years been working to capture and hold the high ground of our culture and from these lofty heights have been able to control discourse and political agenda of our country. Those of us who hold to a Christian worldview are painted as misfits—a defeated army from a bygone era. Rather than accepting such a dismal view, would it not be better to become "more than conquerors" (Rom. 8:37) and regain the high ground in America? It will be a long and difficult fight, but we can do it. Let's talk about our strategy.

In 1975 Dr. Bill Bright (founder of Campus Crusade for Christ) and Loren Cunningham (founder of Youth with a Mission) were given a vision. They saw a vision of culture comprised of seven "mountains": *family, religion, arts and entertainment, business, education, government,* and *media*. They reasoned that whoever controlled the high ground on these mountains would control the culture. Seeing the rapid deterioration of culture in America, they concluded the problem was because these mountains had been occupied by leaders whose agenda was not built on a foundation of moral character and biblical values. They were convinced that to return the American culture to traditional values,

Christian leaders must first of all control the high ground of the mountain peaks of culture.

In 1996 Dr. Bright spoke to a group of businessmen about the seven mountains of culture. He had come to the conclusion that in order to see lasting, positive change we need to find and disciple people of influence and teach them to use that influence for God. One of the attendees in that meeting was Merrill Oster, a dynamic businessman from Chicago. Dr. Bright's message resonated in his heart. Merrill is a leader and a go-getter. He gathered a group of influential fellow-businessmen in Phoenix (where he spends his winters) and they launched Pinnacle Forum. Merrill had found his high ground. Today Pinnacle Forum has chapters throughout the USA, encouraging each other to become more intentional in using their gifts to have a godly influence on the culture.

A spin-off of Pinnacle Forum in Seattle is C-3 Leaders. It consists of four hundred influential leaders who are growing and developing an effective, culture-impacting organization. Their mission is finding high ground to occupy in the Puget Sound and beyond. The great hope for our future lies in the potential of thousands of Christian leaders scaling the mountain peaks of culture and from that vantage point, restoring the values Jesus taught as a guide to daily living.

Finding your high ground can be as simple as looking for a situation, cause, or business you are passionate about. For example, in the 1950s, Lee MacPherson, a small town grocer in Lewiston, Idaho became concerned that the state was going to legalize gambling as their neighbors in Nevada had done. There was much ongoing discussion about the subject, so he decided to run for the state legislature. Upon being elected, he led the effort to pass laws keeping the gambling interests out. Once the laws were enacted, he retired from the legislature and went back to his grocery business. He had found his high ground and occupied it. Gambling was not allowed in Idaho for the next fifty years!

An investment banker in a large city was recruited by a ministry devoted to helping inner-city youth. Besides donating money, he decided to sponsor a boy on a mission trip to Mexico to build houses for the poor. Taking the boy to the airport, he discovered the young man had never been more than a few miles from his neighborhood, much less on an airplane. Upon returning from the mission, the boy said, "That wasn't much of a house we built for them, was it?"

The banker replied, "No, it wasn't."

The boy continued, "I noticed the mom and dad loved each other and were grateful for the house. I have never seen that before."

The banker pledged to himself, "I will spend the rest of my life helping boys like this one." In so doing, he took a lofty peak.

Norm Evans is a member of the elite profession: football offensive tackle. He played fourteen seasons in the NFL and was selected for two pro-bowl games. He played in three Super Bowls with the Miami Dolphins. He retired in 1978 from the Seattle Seahawks. For many retiring professional athletes, finding another career is challenging. Norm found this to be so until he made a connection with Professional Athletes Outreach, a Christian organization dedicated to serving the needs of families of pro athletes. Norm found his high ground in Outreach, and he spent the rest of his working career helping the families of professional athletes. Because he understood the pressure and stress a high profile career in sports can generate, he was uniquely qualified to serve and assist the family needs of a select group of people. Today there are thousands of families whose lives are more stable because Norm Evans took the high ground on the family mountain of culture. Through retreats, seminars and one-on-one counseling, Norm and his wife Bobbie have taught professional athletes how to live God-centered lives. By building a network of peers who deal with similar problems, they have created a culture of support and education for younger athletes. They operate on the principle that when you help people of influence live godly lives, you will impact our culture with healthy values. They have taken high ground on the family mountain.

Darwin "Cub" Grimm has taken unusual but high ground on the religion mountain. A gifted athlete in his youth, he was a record-setting star in baseball, basketball, and track. He also discovered the value of training with weights in improving athletic performance and overall health. He was called into the ministry and found his high ground by combining his love for sports and weight training with his love for people by putting a weight training area in his church. He recruited guys from the community to work out in his gym. The only condition was they had to attend church once a month. This outreach became his high ground in ministry, and he served many families he would otherwise not have met.

In 1985 Rick Stephens found high ground when he established Horizon Hobby in Champaign, Illinois. His business has become the top company in the world for designing, developing, and marketing radio-controlled planes, cars, helos, and boats. They have over seven hundred employees and several plants around the world. Rick is a strong, committed Christian who has built his business on the principles Jesus taught. Because he is vocal about sharing these culture-changing values, he has had a strong impact on employees, customers, vendors, and other business leaders. Rick also uses the resources of his company to involve others in community service and activities which demonstrate the positive influence of Christianity.

In 1948 Mike Martin had a burden on his heart for educating young people in a Christian environment. He managed to lease the abandoned tuberculosis sanitarium in North Seattle. There he started a high school (King's Garden) that graduated its first class in 1951. Down through the years, King's Schools has grown into a K–12 grade, high-quality Christian school committed to providing an education that teaches values and integrity based on godly principles. The high ground taken by a godly man has been a great blessing to families in North Seattle, and their influence extends throughout the world.

Rick Klopcic and his family have taken high ground on the mountain of arts and entertainment. They operate the Fireside Dinner Theater in Ft. Atkins, Wisconsin. Their wholesome, first-class theater and musical productions plus their wonderful dinners have made them one of the top tourist attractions in the Midwest. Rick begins each performance by welcoming everyone to his family and praying. They are a godly influence in their community and also in the lives of employees, including the talent they recruit from Broadway and the arts community. God has given them a great opportunity to impact an important aspect of culture and to share the profits of their theater, supporting other globally-dynamic Christian ministries.

Joel C. Rosenberg is taking high ground on the media mountain. Joel is a gifted writer who has become an expert observer and writer on the Middle East. His best-selling novels have been a highly effective tool to educate people on how Bible prophecy is playing out in current events.

You are most likely to find your high ground by blooming where you are planted right now. If you grow and get better at whatever you are doing, you may already be in a position to win battles. Be wise and courageous. Do what you are called to do in a way that sets an example of what God can accomplish with a dedicated servant-leader.

Seek God's calling on your life. Is there a place He is speaking to you about? Can you see an area of injustice or need? If something about the culture bothers you, learn more about it, and ask God to lead you to your high ground.

Cemetery Hill was not a massive mountain. It was simply a place of high ground where success was achieved. Winning a war is normally the result of a lot of small victories that add up. To change our culture, we need to dominate many small hills. Jesus said, "A city that is set on a hill cannot be hidden" (Matt. 5:14). From the high ground of the hilltop, we can show our communities the values of Jesus by the way we live.

The High Ground of Abraham

"Now it came to pass after these things that God tested Abraham, and said to him 'Abraham!' And he said, 'Here I am.' And He said, 'Take your son, your only son Isaac, whom you love, and go to the land of Moriah, and offer him there as a burnt offering on one of the mountains of which I shall tell you.'"

—Genesis 22:1–2

A call to high ground is not always a glorious and joyous occasion. It was certainly not the case for Abraham. His call to high ground was in the form of giving up the one he loved more than anything, his son Isaac.

As I have read and reflected on this story, what amazes me most is that Abraham rose up and started his journey the very next day. The only explanation I can think of for this immediate obedience is that Abram had been following God for one hundred years. He must have learned that God had a plan and reason for everything He did, and though he did not understand, he was willing to trust God.

When they came to the mountain and reached the high ground God had set for him, Abraham built an altar, arranged the wood, took his son, and placed him on the altar.

When he took his knife to slay Isaac, God spoke. He said, "Do not lay your hand on the lad or do anything to him, for now I know that you fear God, since you have not withheld your son, your only son from me" (Gen. 22:12).

God always knows what we love the most, and it seems that is always what God asks us to give up for Him. Finding the high ground in our lives is accompanied with a level of complete surrender to God's will and way. When we are willing to yield, amazing things happen.

"Then the angel of the Lord called to Abraham a second time out of heaven and said, 'By Myself have I sworn,' says the Lord, 'because you have done this thing and have not withheld your son, your only son. In blessing I will bless you and in multiplying I will multiply your descendants as the stars of the heaven and as the sand which is on the seashore; your descendants shall possess the gates of their enemies. In your seed all the nations of the earth shall be blessed, because you have obeyed My voice'" (Gen. 22:15–18).

When we have a high ground experience, God often looks into our heart to see what we love the very most. Then He wants to see if we are willing to give it up to follow Him.

When we give it up, He will then take that seed and multiply it over and over again. The little bit we give up produces a great blessing in the lives of others.

What do you love the most? Has God taken you to high ground and asked you to give it up?

MOSES' HIGH GROUND EXPERIENCE

"So be ready in the morning, and come up in the morning to Mount
Sinai and present yourself to Me there on top of the mountain."
—Exodus 34:2

One of the amazing stories in the Bible is how God used Moses, a
long-term sheep herder, to lead a group of slaves out of Egypt and
build them into a nation. A lot of the time, I am sure Moses felt
like he was still herding sheep. To say that he was in over his head was
probably an understatement. Fortunately, he had some high ground
experiences along the way.

God used Moses and worked through him to accomplish His
purpose. Today God wants to do the same through you. He has a plan
and purpose for your life. Just like Abraham, there is high ground on a
mountain that only you can achieve. The same principles that worked
for Moses can lead you to your service today.

When God spoke to Moses and asked him to make two stone
tablets and join Him on the top of Mount Sinai, He was not making
a suggestion. Moses woke up early the next morning and went up the
mountain as God commanded him to do. Obedience to the known
will of God is the greatest key to being effective and productive as a
Christian.

The Bible says that when Moses made it up the mountain, God
descended, met with Moses, and said to him: "I am the LORD God,
merciful and gracious, long suffering and abounding in goodness and
truth, keeping mercy for thousands, forgiving iniquity and transgres-
sion and sin, by no means clearing the guilty, visiting the iniquity of
the fathers upon the children and children's children to the third and
fourth generation" (Ex. 34:6–7).

Hearing this, Moses bowed down and worshiped. He then asked God, "If now I have found grace in Your sight . . . pardon us our iniquity and sin and take us as Your inheritance" (Ex. 34:9). There, Moses renewed the covenant God had originally made with Abraham.

Leaders go to high ground to fulfill their unique calling. Leaders must be willing to humble themselves before God and ask for forgiveness.

Leaders listen and respond to the direction God gives them. It is vital for a leader to get the details right. Moses returned from the mountain with a game plan (business plan) for the nation of Israel to follow. As history records, when they followed God's plan, they experienced good times and prosperity. When they adapted to the politically correct agenda of their neighboring nations, they experienced oppression and failure. But God was always faithfully to forgive them and give them a new chance when they followed Him.

Have you found high ground like Moses? Are you following a business plan He has given you for your life? Ask God to guide you, and He will do so.

EXECUTIVE PROFILE FOR RALPH H. PALMEN

Mr. Ralph H. Palmen is the founder and president of The Palmen Institute, Inc. and a co-founder of Express Employment Professionals, the nation's largest privately owned employee staffing firm. He has been a professional speaker and consultant to fast growing companies in Europe and North America and has written three books and several training programs on recruiting, hiring, and building companies. He also served as president of Pinnacle Forum, a nonprofit organization that networks high influence leaders and challenges them to use their influence to make a positive impact on the culture. Mr. Palmen serves on the Foundation Board of Northwest Nazarene University and has been active in fund raising for organizations such as Children's Hospital in Seattle, Washington. He has a Doctor of Laws Degree from Northwest Nazarene University.

Mr. Palmen was selected one of Seattle's 100 Newsmakers of Tomorrow by *Time* magazine and the Seattle Chamber of Commerce in 1978. He is a graduate of the Realtor's Institute, a Real Estate Broker, and has studied mortgage banking at Michigan State University.

CPSIA information can be obtained
at www.ICGtesting.com
Printed in the USA
FSOW02n2119030516
19981FS